The Ilisu Dam and its Impact on the Mesopotamian Marshes of Iraq

International Water Law

Volumes published in this Brill Research Perspective are listed at *brill.com/rpwl*

The Ilisu Dam and its Impact on the Mesopotamian Marshes of Iraq

Implications for the Future Directions of International Water Law

By

Raquella Moea Thaman

BRILL

LEIDEN | BOSTON

This paperback book edition is simultaneously published as issue 5.4 of *International Water Law*, DOI: 10.1163/23529369-12340020.

Typeface for the Latin, Greek, and Cyrillic scripts: "Brill". See and download: brill.com/brill-typeface.

ISBN 978-90-04-45866-6 (paperback)
ISBN 978-90-04-45868-0 (e-book)

This book is printed on acid-free paper and produced in a sustainable manner.

Contents

In memory of Ms. Fadia Daibes Murad (1966–2009); in recognition of the courage, rigor and dynamic intellect with which she advocated both for fairness in access to shared water resources, and for gender equity in Palestine and the Middle East. May future scholars continue to be inspired by her memory.

The Ilisu Dam and Its Impact on the Mesopotamian Marshes of Iraq: Implications for the Future Directions of International Water Law

Raquella Moea Thaman
University of the Pacific McGeorge School of Law LLM International Water and Environmental Law, Sacramento, CA, USA
r_thaman@u.pacific.edu

Abstract

The law of international watercourses has been successful in providing some measure of assistance in conflict avoidance and resolution. However, evolution of this body of law, which has been gradual in nature, is facing challenges adapting to climate change and its grave consequences. Climate change is causing the glaciers of the world to melt, and resulting in unpredictable shifts in patterns of rainfall, thus seriously impacting shared watercourses. The history and ecology of the Tigris Euphrates Basin, and the issues surrounding Turkey's recent impoundment of water behind the Ilisu Dam on the Tigris, provide an example highlighting such challenges. This monograph argues that international collaboration over transboundary watercourses is imperative for maintaining peace and stability and should force us to think of new ways to address these newly emerging and growing challenges in this field.

Keywords

climate change – collaboration – dams – international water law – Tigris-Euphrates

1 Introduction: Our Stake in Eden

•••

> We forget that the water cycle and the life cycle are one.
>
> JACQUES COUSTEAU

 | DOI:10.1163/9789004458680_002

Water, a prerequisite to all life on Earth, is also a finite resource. Once the determining factor in whether and where human civilization could thrive, it is now moved, drained and stored at will, (and great expense), to allow for the population of Earth's deserts and wetlands alike. Neither created nor destroyed, there is a quantity of about 1,400 million cubic kilometres of water moving through Earth's hydrologic cycle.[1] The molecules that today follow this path from the atmosphere through Earth and back into the atmosphere again are the same that have done so since the age of dinosaurs and before.

Water is unevenly distributed across the globe, and an increasing number of people live without an adequate or clean supply. Rapidly expanding populations as well as shifts in climate patterns are partly to blame for the mismatch between population centres and water supply. The problems caused by these discrepancies are multiplied by war, lack of infrastructure, and the failure of local and regional governments, as well as states, to act collaboratively to address water shortages.

In the south of Iraq, the Tigris and Euphrates Rivers meet and enter the Persian Gulf forming an ancient and once massive delta wetland ecosystem known as the Mesopotamian Marshes. Believed by some to be the location of the Eden of the Christian Bible, some of the earliest evidence of human civilization has been found in this region.[2] These marshes have since supported human populations and provided irreplaceable habitat for numerous plant and animal species. Once thriving bird populations and aquatic life, as well as buffalo, and a number of threatened and endangered species make the marshes their home. The health of the marshes can be seen as a barometer for both the ecological and political health of the region. War and drought are among the culprits that have caused their destruction. When the water flows and socio-political factors are tolerable, the marshes recover and again become capable of supporting life.

The southern portion of the Tigris Euphrates River Basin is dry. The rivers that bring water to the marshes are fed primarily by winter rains and the melting snow and glaciers on distant mountain ranges located across international

1 T. Loftas, 'Water a fine resource', in *Dimensions of Need: An Atlas of Food and Agriculture* (Rome: Food and Agriculture Organization of the United Nations, 1995), http://www.fao.org/3/u8480e/U8480E0c.htm#Where%20the%20water%20is, all websites accessed 1 December 2020 unless otherwise noted.

2 D. O. Edzard, et al., '*History of Mesopotamia*', Encyclopedia Britannica Online (22 October 2019), https://www.britannica.com/place/Mesopotamia-historical-region-Asia.

borders. These rivers provide most of the region's water and without their flow, there would be virtually none. Iraq, for example, is 95% dependent on the rivers for its agricultural and industrial needs and 85% dependent on them for its domestic needs.[3] The primary riparian states to the waters of the Tigris and Euphrates are Turkey, Syria and Iraq. Iran shares in the waters of the Tigris only. Saudi Arabia and Jordan share in smaller part the waters of the Euphrates at 1.9% and .03% respectively.[4] Because of both climatological changes and uncoordinated, unilaterally devised human activity, there is already an insufficient supply of water to meet the needs of the people and sustain the ecosystems of the region.[5]

Iraq is running out of water. According to its Planning Ministry, about 90% of the country is now desert and farmland is disappearing at the rate of 5% per year.[6] The water shortage in Iraq is severe. The flow of the rivers has decreased by 40% over the last 20 years. Partly to blame are dams that have been built upstream in Turkey, and the debate over Turkey's obligations with regard to the water crisis in Iraq is far from resolved. There are indeed other factors affecting the supply of water, and therein lies the rub. Turkey's recent completion of the Ilisu Dam and the impounding of water behind it threaten to further tighten the flow of water to Iraq. While Turkey claims that what it calls a comparatively minimal withdrawal of water from the Tigris cannot be blamed for the ultimate destruction of the marshes, it may also be that increment that pushes this unique ecosystem, along with the habitability of the region, over the brink.

In 2010 Turkey began building the Ilisu Dam on the Tigris River.[7] Planned in the 1950s but tied up in legal battles for decades,[8] it is considered part of the South Eastern Anatolia Project, ('GAP'), which is a series of projects on the Tigris and Euphrates Rivers originally designed to facilitate development in the

3 G. R. Pring & B. S. Banaei, 'Tigris and Euphrates Rivers', *Max Planck Encyclopedia of Public International Law* (Oxford: Oxford University Press, 2008).

4 Food and Agriculture Organization of the United Nations (FAO), 'Euphrates-Tigris River Basin', FAO Aquastat (2009), http://www.fao.org/nr/water/aquastat/basins/euphrates-tigris/Euphrates.tigris-CP_eng.pdf, accessed 21 October 2020 [FAO Aquastat].

5 I. Kaya, '*The Euphrates-Tigris Basin: An Overview and Opportunities for Cooperation under International Law*', 44 Arid Lands Newsletter (Fall/Winter 1998), https://cals.arizona.edu/OALS/ALN/aln44/kaya.html.

6 R. Matheson, '*Iraq Close to Running Out of Water*', Al Jazeera (18 September 2018), https://www.aljazeera.com/videos/2018/09/18/iraq-close-to-running-out-of-water/#:~:text=Iraq%20is%20running%20out%20of,by%20five%20percent%20each%20year.

7 N. Bremer, *The Regulation of the Non-Navigational use of the Euphrates and Tigris River System* (The Hague: Eleven International Publishing, 2017), at 257.

8 P. Sevinclidir, '*Hasankeyf: Ancient Town in Turkey Faces Dam Flood*', BBC News Online (2 February 2016), https://www.bbc.com/news/world-middle-east-35471815.

southeast region of Turkey. The Ilisu Dam represents one of the largest and most controversial projects of the GAP to date. The project has generated such extraordinary controversy because of its likely ecological, humanitarian and cultural impacts. In July 2019, satellite images indicated that Turkey had begun to impound water behind the dam and the global community continued to struggle to find a way to ameliorate these impacts.[9] Two major areas of controversy have taken centre stage. Behind the dam, in Turkey, lies the 12,000-year-old city of Hasankeyf. It is one of the oldest continually inhabited human settlements in the world.[10] Opponents of the dam project estimated that nearly 80,000 people would be displaced and that one of the world's most precious archaeological treasures would be destroyed.[11]

Of primary concern for this monograph, however, is the search for an adequate legal framework for addressing the downstream impact on the Mesopotamian Marshes of Iraq and the people that depend on those marshes. The existing legal regime governing the use of the waters of the Tigris River provides scant protection against the potential harm caused by the dam.

Climate change is causing glaciers the world over to melt and causing unpredictable shifts in rainfall patterns. The forces of nature that were once predictable, even if harsh, are no longer the dependable source of life-giving resources they once were. The spring floods have been tamed by human intervention, and now the accumulation of snow that once fed those floods is being replaced by rain that runs its course as soon as it reaches the earth.

More than ever, international collaboration in the use of transboundary watercourses is imperative for maintaining peace and stability in regions already struggling with scarcity. Running headlong into any international effort at resolution is the recent rise of nationalism and its elevation of state sovereignty over good neighbourliness and collaboration. The interests at stake are global, however. In the case of the Tigris/Euphrates (TE) basin, the preservation of a peoples' ability to survive in their home region, along with the preservation of the international treasure of the Mesopotamian Marshes, has clear global benefits. Given the inadequacy of the current legal regime, are there existing models that can be replicated?

---

9 A. Kucukgocmen, '*Turkey Starts Filling Huge Tigris River Dam, Activists Say*', Reuters (2 August 2019), https://www.reuters.com/article/us-turkey-dam/turkey-starts-filling-huge-tigris-river-dam-activists-say-idUSKCN1US194.

10 K. Patel, '*Slowly Flooding History*', NASA Earth Observatory (2020), https://earthobservatory.nasa.gov/images/146439/slowly-flooding-history, accessed 25 September 2020.

11 C. Letsch, '*Turkey's 12,000 Year Old Hasankeyf Settlement Faces Obliteration*', The Guardian (29 August 2017).

Preliminarily, this monograph will outline the global water resources situation and then examine the hydrogeography of the Tigris Euphrates region along with the history of water use in the Tigris Euphrates River Basin and its impact on the Mesopotamian Marshes. Then the impacts of climate change, mismanagement, acts of war and major water projects on the river will be examined. The potential additional impact of the filling of the Ilisu Dam will then be assessed in light of already existing problems. The legal regimen of the Tigris Euphrates River Basin will be examined to determine what, if any, rights or obligations the riparian nations might have with regard to each other and what kinds of new approaches could be expanded to increase collaboration. The topic of collaborative problem solving in the sharing of international resources will then be discussed in light of the promising example of the Senegal River Basin. A comparative snapshot of three other transboundary water conflicts will shed some light on the underlying factors hindering regional collaboration. In conclusion, the need for concerted global intervention to maintain the liveability of Earth and increase resilience in the face of the rapidly changing availability of resources will be explored and the clear need for a unified collaborative approach to such intervention reiterated.

2 Eden in the Anthropocene

•••

> Rivers know this, there is no hurry, we shall get there someday.
>
> A. A. MILNE

∴

Water covers about 75% of the Earth's surface. Of this, a surprisingly minute amount, only one hundredth of one percent, is available for human consumption.[12] Over 97.5% is in the ocean and most of the remaining 2.5% is trapped in (rapidly melting) glaciers or in groundwater.[13] With the possible exception of some reservoirs of fossil water deep beneath Earth's crust, every drop of water has been consumed by some form of life and then returned to

12 Loftas, *supra* note 1.

13 *Id.*

the hydrologic cycle to be again consumed and returned. Water is not fixed to a geographic location. It moves through the atmosphere and soil alike moving around the globe on a continuous journey. How water originally came to Earth is uncertain, however some scientists believe water was first delivered to Earth via comet or asteroid.[14]

A finite resource in constant motion around the globe, water may be flowing in the Nile one year and the Tigris another. The same drops may be extracted by a multinational conglomerate from a precious supply in India one year and the next year treated and released into Lake Michigan in the United States. Since the earliest engineers began to move water to quench their thirst in the desert and to build dikes to hold back the seasonal deluge, humans have untethered their water supply from its natural state in terms of its source, its natural flow and its duration in a particular location.

Milne's quote seems to refer to the notion that Nature follows its own course and that humans must learn to 'go with the flow'. This romantic ideal that humans are a part of, and should try to live in harmony with, Nature is perhaps no longer attainable.

'Something's happened to the plumbing'.[15] The Anthropocene is the name given to the most recent geologic epoch in which human influences rather than geologic forces have taken over as the dominant influence on Earth.[16] Geologists have not decided exactly when the Anthropocene began. There are several markers of human influence to consider. Some would argue that it began with the Industrial Revolution, others with the advent of plastics. One might also consider that the Anthropocene began with the human ability to create and control fire. Another potential marker could be the development of antibiotics and other improvements in medicine that have greatly improved human survival. We now exist in a time where natural forces have been permanently altered as a side effect of our activity. Rather than a declaration of victory over Nature, calling this epoch the Anthropocene is a realization that we have unwittingly and possibly permanently disrupted the very systems

14 B. Greene, '*How Did Water Come to Earth?*' Smithsonian Magazine (May 2013), https://www.smithsonianmag.com/science-nature/how-did-water-come-to-earth-72037248/.

15 California Governor Gavin Newsom, in September 2020, explaining to U.S. President Donald Trump the relationship between the increasingly catastrophic fires of recent years and climate change. A. Koseff, '*Trump Dismisses Newsom's Climate Warning, Biden Goes on Attack over California Fires*', San Francisco Chronicle (14 September 2020), https://www.sfchronicle.com/politics/article/Newsom-Trump-to-meet-on-California-fires-in-15565541.php.

16 J. Myers, '*What is the Anthropocene? And Why Does it Matter?*', World Economic Forum (31 August 2016), https://www.weforum.org/agenda/2016/08/what-is-the-anthropocene-and-why-does-it-matter/, accessed 8 October 2020.

that have made our planet habitable. It is no longer possible to simply stop the harmful activity and wait for a recovery.

The term 'ecosystem services' refers to the natural processes we depend on to meet any number of needs and ultimately to ensure our survival.[17] They are the 'direct and indirect contributions of ecosystems to human wellbeing'.[18] The air we breathe is produced by the respiratory process of living plants in our ecosystems. Our food is dependent on vastly more complicated systems.

The extent of human interference has in many cases so dramatically altered the functioning of ecosystems that they no longer can provide the services that support life on Earth. Increasingly, human intervention will be necessary to maintain the existence of numerous species, and ultimately, the life support systems of Earth. Ecosystem restoration, maintenance, rehabilitation and other human interventions could be said to fall under the broader umbrella term of intervention ecology.[19] Rather than an attempt to 'turn the clock back' to some indeterminate time in history or to 'some imagined Eden', intervention ecology refers to the set of human actions necessary to ensure continued delivery of ecosystem services.[20] Where rivers have been dammed, for example, the nutrient rich silt is trapped behind the dam and those nutrients must be replaced though human intervention to maintain the viability of agriculture downstream. In order to restore fish populations where fish ladders have been installed and migratory fish populations begin to return to old runs, the gravel of the riverbed, necessary for spawning, must be continually replaced as the natural material remains trapped behind the dam.[21] Where coral reefs have been decimated, the hulls of old ships are sometimes sunken to provide alternate habitat for the fish dependent on the reefs.[22] Scientists

17 FAO, 'Ecosystem Services & Biodiversity (ESB)', http://www.fao.org/ecosystem-services-biodiversity/en, accessed 7 December 2020.

18 Services have been divided into four categories: 'provisioning services' which are those that provide food, water and shelter; 'regulating services' which are those that provide such things as climate regulation and water purification; 'habitat services' that support biodiversity; and 'cultural services' that support non-material benefits people derive from ecosystems such as recreation and aesthetic values. European Parliament Briefing Ecosystem Services Valuing our Natural Capital, https://www.europarl.europa.eu/RegData/etudes/BRIE/2015/551321/EPRS_BRI(2015)551321_EN.pdf, accessed 7 December 2020.

19 R. J. Hobbs, '*Intervention Ecology: Applying Ecological Science in the Twenty-first Century*', 61(6) *BioScience* (2011) 442–450, at 442.

20 *Id.*

21 Trinity River Restoration Program, 'Gravel Augmentation', https://www.trrp.net/restoration/gravel-augmentation/, accessed 16 August 2020.

22 A. Taylor, '*Artificial Reefs around the World*', The Atlantic (2011).

are now able to use 3-D printing technology to more accurately duplicate the textures of the reef thereby hopefully making a more effective repair.[23]

After the destruction of the Mesopotamian Marshes by Saddam Hussein, dedicated environmentalists worked to restore them with startling success. As the millennia of fossilized life is extracted from the soil beneath the marshes, its continued burning and contribution to climate change accelerates the ecological changes affecting the marshes. Now with droughts and decreased flows due to a multitude of factors, the marshes have once again shrunk to one quarter their original size. The loss of the spring floods has resulted in a loss of turbidity in the water and consequent reduction in the fertile silt characteristic of the marshes. It has also resulted in an increase in saltwater intrusion into the marshes causing severe problems, including complete changes in fish populations and the death of the water buffalo that depend on the marshes for water. Artificial flood simulations are being engineered to combat saltwater intrusion. This is a partial solution and does nothing to address the absence of the nutrient rich silt that once supported plant life in the area. Global ecosystem services, such as the storage of fresh water in mountain glaciers for use in the summer, the regulation of water and air temperatures by the great ice sheets, and others, must be maintained on a global scale. These services are infinitely interconnected with global systems that do not recognize political boundaries. In order to intervene effectively, transboundary collaboration aimed at addressing common goals in the maintenance and retention of global ecosystem services is imperative. The model provided by the Senegal River Basin countries is a hopeful one. With regard to Earth's water supply, the community of interest is global as is the responsibility for its stewardship. When there is simply not enough water in a river for all riparian states to protect their ecosystems and provide a reasonable quality of life for their people, and an underlying cause is climate change, the solutions require a global response rather than an exacerbation of local tensions that are older than the very notion to burn ancient accumulations of carbon for energy. Our legal systems are not designed to address the possibility that the process of remediating ecological damage might need to continue indefinitely.[24] Whether we have the philosophical, legal and technological competence to move from being stewards of natural systems to being engineers of artificial systems designed

23 L. Parker, '*3D-Printed Reefs Offer Hope in Coral Bleaching Crisis*', National Geographic (2017).

24 M. A. Palmer & J. B. Ruhl, '*Aligning Restoration Science and the Law to Sustain Ecological Infrastructure for the Future*', 13(9) Frontiers in Ecology and the Environment (2015) 512–519.

to replace those we have destroyed is to be determined. From adding gravel back to a starved riverbed to sinking derelict ships for replacement of coral reefs, humans are having to fill in for the ecosystem services we once took for granted.

Our metaphors are losing validity. Milne's quote urges patience and solace in the recognition that there are forces greater than ourselves. Now we, as humans, have taken our place among those forces, and the consequences are unfathomable. One must hope that if we move quickly enough, we may be able to once again someday let go of the tiller and allow the river to take us on its journey.

3 The Tigris Euphrates River Basin

•••

> A river flowed out of Eden to water the garden, and there it divided and became four rivers. The name of the first is the Pishon. It is the one that flowed around the whole land of Havilah, where there is gold. And the gold of that land is good; bdellium and onyx stone are there. The name of the second river is the Gihon. It is the one that flowed around the whole land of Cush. And the name of the third river is the Tigris, which flows east of Assyria. And the fourth river is the Euphrates. The Lord God took the man and put him in the garden of Eden to work it and keep it.
>
> GENESIS 2:10–15, BIBLE

∴

3.1 *The Water of the Tigris Euphrates River Basin*

3.1.1 The Hydro-Geography of the Tigris Euphrates River Basin

Forming the largest river basin in southwest Asia, the Tigris and Euphrates Rivers are for the most part separate systems until they meet at Al Qurnah, Iraq, before flowing into the Persian Gulf. Whether or not the rivers are part of a single basin is disputed by some, but it is often treated as one.[25]

25 S. C. McCaffrey, *The Law of International Watercourses* (Oxford: Oxford University Press, 2007), at 324.

As a transboundary basin, it covers an area of 879,790 square kilometres, nearly half of which (46%) lies in Iraq.[26] The rest is distributed between Turkey, Iran, Syria, Saudi Arabia and Jordan. The Tigris and Euphrates (TE) River Basin stretches from the Taurus mountain range of southeast Turkey in the north, to the Mesopotamian Marshes of Iraq in the south, and from the Zagros Mountains of Iran in the east, to Syria in the west. Saudi Arabia and Jordan share only small portions of the river.[27] About two thirds the length of both rivers run through the mountains of Turkey and the high plateaus of Iraq and Syria before they flow into the plains of Mesopotamia, through the Mesopotamian Marshes, and finally into the Persian Gulf. About 190 kilometres before flowing into the Gulf, the rivers converge to form a single flow called the Shatt Al-Arab.[28] Just before entering the Gulf, the Shatt Al-Arab is joined by the Karun River, which originates in Iran and carries a mean annual flow of 24.7 cubic kilometres of water. Further upstream, the Euphrates and Tigris are also connected by several canals used to transfer water between the two rivers.[29]

3.1.2 The Rivers

The sources of both the Tigris and Euphrates, the mighty rivers that formed the cradle of western civilization, are located just 50 miles apart in the mountains of Eastern Turkey.[30] These mountains and their glaciers are the source of the water that has sustained civilizations for thousands of years. The Tigris begins at Lake Hazar in the Taurus mountains of eastern Turkey not far from where the Euphrates River is formed at the confluence of two mountain rivers, the Murat and the Karasu in the area between the Black Sea and Lake Van.[31] These rivers are fed by winter snow melt from the peaks of Mount Ararat. Believed by some biblical scholars to be the final resting place of Noah's Ark, Mount Ararat's cultural as well as ecological significance cannot be underestimated.[32]

The rivers diverge as they leave the mountains and have a span of about 250 miles between them at the Turkish Syrian border. Flowing into Syria after passing through the Turkish city of Birecik, the Euphrates is then joined by two

26 FAO Aquastat, *supra* note 4.
27 *Id.*
28 *Id.*
29 *Id.*
30 L. Owen et al., '*Tigris-Euphrates River System*', Encyclopedia Britannica Online (20 January 2016), https://www.britannica.com/place/Tigris-Euphrates-river-system.
31 FAO Aquastat, *supra* note 4.
32 Editors, '*Mount Ararat*', Encyclopedia Britannica Online (23 October 2019), https://www.britannica.com/place/Mount-Ararat, accessed 25 September 2020.

major tributaries, the Khabur and the Balik, which also originate in Turkey.[33] The river then flows through Syria and into Iraq.

Although shorter than the Euphrates, the Tigris carries more water.[34] Both receive most of their water from annual snowmelt, and both rivers enter a joint aquifer upstream from where they meet.[35] There is wide variation in the flow of both rivers due to climatic changes as well as human interference with the rivers.[36] In terms of discharge, the Tigris has a mean annual flow of 42,230 million cubic meters, with a minimum of 5,140 and a maximum of 440,000 per year.[37]

While the Euphrates enters Syria for a short time, the Tigris 'never enters it entirely; it forms the border of that country with Turkey for some 40 km before entering Iraq'.[38] The Tigris receives about 51% of its water from Turkey, 39% from Iraq, and the remaining 10% from Iran.[39]

After the Tigris leaves Turkey, it is fed by numerous tributaries that increase its flow as it makes its way to the Persian Gulf. Tributaries from the Zagros Mountains in Iran 'contribute importantly' to the Tigris.[40] The Tigris receives a large amount of water from the Greater Zab, the Lesser Zab, the Adhaim and the Diyala, which are among many other smaller tributaries that feed into it from the Taurus-Zagros mountain range.[41] The amount at the city of Kut in Iraq is currently 26 billion cubic metres, with variation between dry and wet seasons.[42] There are currently 14 dams on the Tigris.[43]

The source of much of the Basin's water supply is disappearing. Because of climate change, Turkey's glaciers are vanishing. Over the last forty years, Turkey's glaciated area has decreased in size by more than half and five of its

---

33 FAO Aquastat, *supra* note 4.

34 N. E. Ohara et al., '*Water Balance Study for the Tigris-Euphrates River Basin*', 16(12) Journal of Hydrologic Engineering (2011) 1071–1082.

35 FAO Aquastat, *supra* note 4.

36 A. Kirschner & K. Tiroch, '*The Waters of the Euphrates and Tigris: An International Law Perspective*', 16 Max Planck Yearbook of United Nations Law (2012) 329–394.

37 T. M. Naff, *Water in the Middle East* (Boulder: Westview Press, 1984).

38 McCaffrey (2007), *supra* note 25, at 324.

39 FAO Aquastat, *supra* note 4.

40 McCaffrey (2007), *supra* note 25, at 324.

41 Naff, *supra* note 37, at 85.

42 United Nations Economic and Social Commission for Western Asia (UN-ESCWA) & Bundesanstalt für Geowissenschaften und Rohstoffe (BGR), *Inventory of Shared Water Resources in Western Asia* (Beirut: UN-ESCWA and BGR, 2013), at 101, http://waterinventory.org/sites/waterinventory.org/files/00-inventory-of-shared-water-resources-in-western-asia-web.pdf.

43 *Id.* at 101.

glaciers have disappeared entirely.[44] The source of the rivers, Mount Ararat, is a dormant stratovolcano consisting of two peaks, the highest of which rises to nearly 17,000 feet.[45] The highest mountain in Turkey, Ararat, and its smaller neighbour Uludoruk, are home to the two main glaciers left in Turkey.[46] Theses glaciers function as the water storage mechanism for the TE Basin.

The majority of Earth's fresh water, about three quarters, is stored in glacial ice.[47] It is melting snow from these glaciers that feeds the rivers after the spring rains have ceased. As global temperatures increase and this glacial melting continues, it is likely to result in initially higher spring flooding as the water from the glacial melt is amplified by the winter and spring rains. When the climate has become too warm to form any ice, the water will no longer be stored in the winter for gradual distribution during the drier months.[48] The rain falling in the Turkish highlands will simply flow directly to the sea, possibly leaving the Basin completely dry in the summer months. These factors present an existential threat to populations and ecosystems depending on the TE Basin's water supply. They are also factors cited in support of the construction of upstream dams on the rivers.[49]

3.1.3 Climate

The climate of the majority of the TE Basin is characterized as a sub-tropical Mediterranean climate with dry summers and with nearly all of the precipitation occurring in the winter.[50] The upper basin, at higher altitudes, has cold winters with much of the precipitation occurring as snow in winter and rain in the spring. The climate of the area comprising the lower TE River Basin is

44 L. Rocchio, '*Turkish Glaciers Shrink by Half*', NASA Global Climate Change (1 July 2015), https://climate.nasa.gov/news/2304/turkish-glaciers-shrink-by-half/, accessed 25 September 2020.

45 *Id.*

46 *Id.*

47 U.S. Geological Survey (USGS), 'How Much of the Earth's Water is Stored in Glaciers?', https://www.usgs.gov/faqs/how-much-earths-water-stored-glaciers?qt-news_science_products=0#qt-news_science_products, accessed 25 September 2020.

48 USGS, 'What are the Impacts of Glacier Loss, Other than Losing an Aesthetic Landscape Feature?', https://www.usgs.gov/faqs/what-are-impacts-glacier-loss-other-losing-aesthetic-landscape-feature?qt-news_science_products=0#qt-news_science_products, accessed 25 September 2020.

49 P. Brown, '*Dam Backup Plan for Glacier Ice Loss*', Climate News Network (1 June 2016), https://climatenewsnetwork.net/dam-back-up-plan-for-glacier-ice-loss/; see also E. Roston & Bloomberg, '*While Most Industries Suffer Due to the Climate Crisis, Hydropower Sees Opportunities*', Fortune (17 November 2019), https://fortune.com/2019/11/17/climate-change-effects-melting-glaciers-dams-hydropower-freshwater-storage/.

50 FAO Aquastat, *supra* note 4.

arid. Iraq's mean annual precipitation is 7.6 inches, with almost all of that falling from December through February.[51] The winters are generally cool and the summers range from hot to extremely hot.[52]

Drought is not uncommon in the lower TE Basin. Until recently, the region encompassing Iraq and Syria has been suffering through an extended period without its usual rainfall. In addition to the frequency of drought in the region, some scholars believe that the entire region may be becoming warmer and drier as a more permanent climatic trend.[53] In 2018, the ongoing severe drought in Iraq caused water levels to drop to the degree that ruins of the ancient Mitanni civilization, about 3400 years old, were revealed as the waters of the Tigris receded, lowering the level of the Mosul reservoir.[54] The lower TE Basin region is also affected by dry dust wind systems called the South and Southeasterly Sharqui, and also by the North and Northwest Shamal that contribute to extensive surface heating.[55] These winds can blow for several days at a time, creating sand and dust storms with a force powerful enough to cause major damage, for example, uprooting trees and decimating crops.

3.2 *Early History of Water Use*

Mesopotamia, taking its name from the Greek 'mesos' meaning middle, and 'potamos' meaning river, is the location of some of the world's oldest civilizations. The river basin of the Tigris and Euphrates, comprising much of what has been known as the 'Fertile Crescent', provided the resources necessary for the development of these early civilizations. From what has been called the 'Cradle of Civilization' comes some of the earliest recorded stories of the ancient Sumerian people, which tell about the great floods that were viewed as sources of both destruction and cleansing. The technologically advanced culture of ancient Sumer developed extensive systems of canals for flood control, irrigation and the transport of the excess food produced through the irrigation to other areas.[56] The success of these systems allowed for the establishment of agriculture in areas without enough rainfall to otherwise grow crops. It was

51 World Bank Group, Climate Change Knowledge Portal, 'Iraq: Climate Data', https://climateknowledgeportal.worldbank.org/country/iraq/climate-data-historical#.

52 *Id.*

53 K. Nasser, '*The Modality of Climate Change in the Middle East, Drought or Drying Up?*', 2(1) Journal of Interrupted Studies (2019) 118–140.

54 K. Epstein, '*A Drought Revealed a Palace Thousands of Years Old Submerged in an Iraq Reservoir*', The Washington Post (30 June, 2019).

55 World Bank Group, *supra* note 52.

56 T. Jacobsen & R. Adams, '*Salt and Silt in Ancient Mesopotamia*', 128(3334) Science (21 November 1958) 1251–1257.

also the success of these systems' ability to move water that was in part responsible for the eventual decline in agriculture. As the water evaporated from the irrigated soils, the salts left behind rendered the soils infertile.[57]

As early as 8000 BCE the shift from hunting and gathering had begun, and agriculturally-based communities were established in northern Mesopotamia.[58] About two millennia later, communities that had developed irrigation systems rather than depending on rainfall were able to establish settlements further to the south.[59] These technologies, in allowing human settlements to be established in the more arid regions of Mesopotamia themselves then became indispensable as those populations grew. These projects, which required massive amounts and coordination of human labour to build, perhaps facilitated, and were likewise facilitated by, the rise of centralized systems of governance and the transition from democratic systems of decision-making to stratified hierarchical governments.

These early empires developed customary legal systems that were focused on assigning responsibility for the maintenance of these canals and for the assessment of liability in the event of their failure.[60] Under these systems anyone who failed to maintain their canal and thereby caused damage to another's property would be required to 'restore the status quo ante'.[61] However, as important as the management of water was for these early civilizations, there is little in the known record of formal law addressing the matter.[62] The Code of Hammurabi, rediscovered in 1901 and dating to the mid-1700s BCE addressed the use and management of water in only four of its 282 articles.[63] Article 53 provides: 'If anyone be too lazy to keep his dam in proper condition, and does not so keep it; if then the dam break and all the fields be flooded, then shall he in whose dam the break occurred be sold for money, and the money shall replace the corn which he has caused to be ruined'. Article 54 provides: 'If he be not able to replace the corn, then he and his possessions shall be divided among the farmers whose corn he has flooded'. Article 55 provides: 'If any one open his ditches to water his crop, but is careless, and the water flood the field

57 *Id.*

58 The Metropolitan Museum of Art, 'Mesopotamia, 8000–2000 B.C.', https://www.metmuseum.org/toah/ht/02/wam.html, accessed 26 September 2020.

59 *Id.*

60 I. Kornfeld, '*Mesopotamia: A History of Water and Law*', in J. Dellapenna & J. Gupta (eds.), *The Evolution of the Law and Politics of Water* (Cham: Springer, 2009), 21–26 at 21.

61 *Id.*

62 *Id.*, at 28.

63 L. W. King (translator), *The Code of Hammurabi*, The Avalon Project, Yale Law School Lillian Goldman Law Library, https://avalon.law.yale.edu/ancient/hamframe.asp, accessed 26 September 2020.

of his neighbor, then he shall pay his neighbor corn for his loss'. Article 56 provides: 'If a man let in the water, and the water overflow the plantation of his neighbor, he shall pay ten gur of corn for every ten gan of land'.[64] Other ancient legal systems, that of the Hittites, for example, provide similar codes for assigning liability.

4 The Mesopotamian Marshes

The ecological, cultural and historical significance of the Mesopotamian Marshes cannot be overstated. Some scholars believe that the garden of Eden from the biblical creation story was actually the Mesopotamian Marshes. The four rivers of Eden are thought by some to include the Euphrates, the Tigris and the Karun. A barometer for the ecological and socio-political health of the region, the marshes and their survival serve to provide a case in point for the exploration of the way in which transboundary resources can be shared. Their physical characteristics, significant contribution to human history, and ecological importance make them a global asset deserving of international concern.

4.1 *Physical Characteristics*

At the confluence of the Tigris and Euphrates, the Mesopotamian Marshes supported the birth of human civilization and have sustained human populations for thousands of years. Once comprising an area of more than 17,000 square kilometres,[65] they were even estimated to be as much as twice that size as late as 1985.[66] 'The Marshes were a once vast oasis of reedy swampland, 'hawrs', which, probably, since early times, have served as an area of refuge for oppressed and displaced peoples'.[67] '[H]ome to ancient communities for more than five millenia,'[68] the marshes have supported a rich cultural heritage. The Ma'dan people who are believed to be the descendants of the ancient Sumerians lived in the marshes and sustained a unique culture based on their

---

64 *Id.*

65 FAO, 'Iraq', FAO Aquastat (2008), http://www.fao.org/nr/water/aquastat/countries_regions/irq/IRQ-CP_eng.pdf, accessed 26 September 2020.

66 United States Institute of Peace (USIP), '*The Marsh Arabs of Iraq: Hussein's Lesser Known Victims*', Press Release (25 November 2002), https://www.usip.org/press/2002/11/marsh-arabs-iraq-husseins-lesser-known-victims, accessed 27 September 2020.

67 Edzard, D. O. et al., '*Mesopotamia to the End of the Old Babylonian Period*', Encyclopedia Britannica Online (22 October 2019), https://www.britannica.com/place/Mesopotamia-historical-region-Asia#ref55481.

68 S. Kubba, *The Iraqui Marshlands and the Marsh Arabs* (Trans Pacific Press, 2011), at 6.

aquatic environment.[69] Researchers have, in fact, used a study of the Y chromosome and the mitochondrial DNA of the current residents of the marshes to show that they are the descendants of the people of ancient Sumer.[70]

Representing a distinct ecosystem, the marshes are also the life support system for numerous plant and animal species. A profusion of wildlife, including millions of birds, once made the marshes their permanent home, with millions more utilizing it as an important stop on the migratory route between Siberia and Africa.[71] A survey from the 1970s indicated that there were at least 80 species of birds, including some thought to be close to extinction, which inhabited the marshes.[72] Inscribed on the UNESCO World Heritage List in 2016, the 'outstanding universal value' of the marshlands has been formally recognized.[73] Whether or not this recognition can contribute to the restoration and protection of the marshes is uncertain. Over the last few decades, the marshes have been destroyed and then restored, and are now facing destruction yet again.

In addition to supporting its own unique ecosystem and cultural heritage, the health of these and other coastal marshes provides another significant global benefit. Coastal marshland provides an extremely effective carbon sink that can sequester carbon at a much faster rate than Earth's forests.[74] Wetland soils, when healthy, are able to store some of the largest amounts of soil carbon.[75] However, there have been a number of events throughout the last several decades that have damaged the ecosystem of the marshes. Some of these are hopefully isolated events that will never be repeated, and some are

69 N. K. Al-Ansari, S. Knutsson & A. A. Ali, '*Restoring the Garden of Eden, Iraq*', 2(1) Journal of Earth Sciences and Geotechnical Engineering (2012) 53–88.

70 N. E. Al-Zahery et al., '*In Search of the Genetic Footprints of Sumerians: A Survey of Y Chromosome and mtDNA Variation in the Marsh Arabs of Iraq*', 11 BMC Evolutionary Biology (2011) article number 288.

71 C. H. Richardson & N. A. Hussain, 'Restoring the Garden of Eden: An Ecological Assessment of the Marshes of Iraq', 56(6) *BioScience* (2006) 477–489, at 477.

72 *Id.*, at 478.

73 United Nations Educational, Scientific and Cultural Organization (UNESCO), *Report of the Decisions adopted during the 40th session of the World Heritage Committee (Istanbul/ UNESCO, 2016)*, Doc. WHC/16/40.COM/19 (15 November 2016), Decision: 40 COM 8B.16, at 201–205.

74 U.S. National Oceanic and Atmospheric Administration (NOAA), 'What is Blue Carbon?', https://oceanservice.noaa.gov/facts/bluecarbon.html.

75 A. M. Nahlik & M. S. Fennessy, '*Carbon Storage in US Wetlands*', 7 Nature Communications (2016) article number 13835, at 2. Ironically, some of the destruction of the marshes has been for oil exploration. Could it be possible that in a region where so much of the oil responsible for climate change has been extracted, and so much blood has been shed over those oil resources, there is also the potential for a movement toward reversal of the damage through restoration of the marshes?

associated with the ongoing and seemingly intractable problems of managing water resources in the face of climate change and of supporting a population in a desert combat zone.

4.2 *A Catalogue of Water Problems*

The health and the existence of the Mesopotamian Marshes are under threat and with it is the health and survival of the Iraqi people. During the summer of 2018, the Mesopotamian Marshes shrank to about a quarter of their original size. That same summer, over 100,000 people in Basra, the largest city in southern Iraq and its main hub of oil production,[76] fell ill after being poisoned by the city's water supply.[77] This catastrophic event has been attributed to a set of factors, including a severe and prolonged drought, more than 30 years of water mismanagement in Iraq, and the deceased flow of water into Iraq.[78] The following set of problems compound the effect of the large water projects discussed in the subsequent section.

4.2.1 Drought

For about the last two decades, the fertile crescent has been suffering through an extreme drought. For several years, the usual winter rains did not come, and the agricultural regions of northern Iraq and Syria experienced declines in food production.[79] According to NASA the most recent drought in the Eastern Mediterranean region began in 1998 and is the worst in 900 years.[80] Some scholars theorize, however, that the climatic situation in the Middle East is not a drought, and rather a more permanent shift to an even hotter and more arid climate, making the need to develop strategies for managing vital resources all the more urgent. 'Long-term drought in MENA [Middle East and North Africa] has created a new climatic and environmental condition that is quite different from the normal climate in the Middle East. However, some suggest that this new situation is not abnormal but should rather be considered as a new

76 Reuters, 'Factbox: Basra, Oil Hub of Iraq' (December 16 2007), https://www.reuters.com/article/us-iraq-basra-oil/factbox-basra-oil-hub-of-iraq-idUSL1666117420071216.

77 BBC (Director), *Our Water Pollution is a Cancer* [Motion Picture] (2019).

78 W. Belkis, *Basra is Thirsty: Iraq's Failure to Manage the Water Crisis* (Human Rights Watch, 2019).

79 NASA, 'Drought in Iraq', Visible Earth (1 June 2008), https://visibleearth.nasa.gov/view.php?id=8797.

80 K. Hille, '*NASA Finds Drought in Eastern Mediterranean Worst of Past 900 Years*', NASA (1 March 2016), https://www.nasa.gov/feature/goddard/2016/nasa-finds-drought-in-eastern-mediterranean-worst-of-past-900-years.

normality'.[81] Given the possibility of a permanent climatic shift, regional policies would ideally be developed to address the new circumstances.

> However, if it is assumed that the drought is not temporary, that it probably will continue for at least several decades, and that some of its effects are (and will be) irreversible (particularly the possibility of permanent hydrological drought in some areas of the region), it is doubtful whether the term "drought" is appropriate. Future studies could investigate whether what has occurred in the Middle East could be termed "drying up" as a new normality of permanently drier and warmer land has replaced the old one. Due to this epistemological aspect in the study of climate change in the Middle East, this assumption (i.e., drying up rather than drought) is important in its normative implications in that it could change the nature of the governance structure and development targets and policies.[82]

The effects of drought are far reaching. They range from the degradation and salinization of the water supply, desertification of formerly productive land, damage to crops, livestock mortality, and the loss of resources for rural populations resulting in migration.[83] These effects have social and political consequences with even more far reaching ramifications. The resulting crop failures and food shortages have caused a massive rural to urban migration to which some have attributed the unrest leading to the war in Syria.[84] There is a strong link between climate, instability and extremism in the region,[85] and some fear that increased water scarcity will bring a new wave of problems. In September 2018 Basra was the scene of protests, in part, over the lack of clean water.[86] That month at least 12 civilian protesters were killed by security forces trying to disperse the crowds.[87]

---

81 Nasser, *supra* note 54.

82 *Id.*

83 UNESCO, *Integrated Drought Risk Management—National Framework for Iraq* (Baghdad: UNESCO, 2014).

84 H. Fountain, '*Researchers Link Syrian Conflict to a Drought Made Worse by Climate Change*', The New York Times (2 March 2015).

85 AFP, '*Drought Puts Iraq at Risk of More Extremism*', Gulf News (2 September 2018).

86 P. Issa, '*Rains Like no Other: Iraq is Tested in Era of Climate Change*', Associated Press (2 May 2019); see also J. Arraf, '*Months of Protests Roil Iraq's Oil Capital Basra*', National Public Radio (27 September 2018).

87 Arraf, *supra* note 86.

In the spring of 2019, the rains returned reflooding the marshes.[88] Combined with snowmelt from Turkey, both the Tigris and Euphrates, as well as their tributaries, overflowed and flooded the cities and countryside of the Iraqi plains causing damage to crops. Climate change adds another layer of unpredictability to the already untenable system of managing water resources in the lower TE Basin. The region has to be ready for both floods and drought. The activity of Iraq's upstream neighbours is central to its future in terms of both flood control and the presence of adequate water resources.

4.2.2 Poor Water Management and Infrastructure

In addition to drought and reduced supplies of surface water, some of the causes of water shortage in the lower TE Basin and the marshes are due to internal problems. In Iraq, various internal factors account for a reduction in available water and its poor quality. These internal factors, which have devastating effects on Iraq's environment, result from the following practices, including, among others:

- Lack of domestic water usage regulations and/or lack of an enforcement policy for existing regulations
- Lack of a national drought monitoring index to set the guidelines for passing regulations regarding drought monitoring and mitigation, as well as water-related practices affecting surface and groundwater
- Lack of public awareness a well as the absence of effective educational and awareness campaigns to build the knowledge base of the public about responsible water usage and drought preparedness
- Use of old techniques and practices in farming irrigation (for example, flooding rather than using drip irrigation or controlled sprinkler systems)
- Lack of assistance/demonstration/incentive programmes that encourage and promote water conservation/protection practices[89]

In Basra, for example, the problems underlying the inadequate and dangerous water supply are numerous and serve to exacerbate each other. Basra, with its numerous bridges and canals, was once known as the 'Venice of the Middle East' and served as a tourist destination for visitors from the region. The Shatt al-Arab is the primary source of drinking water for the now more than 4 million people of Basra. Fresh water flowing into the Shatt al-Arab has decreased because of both drought conditions and the construction of dams upstream. This has caused the waters of the Gulf of Arabia to intrude and significantly

88 Issa, *supra* note 86.

89 UNESCO (2014), *supra* note 83.

increase the salinity of the water supply.[90] In addition to these problems, an antiquated water infrastructure compounds the problem. Not enough water is supplied to the treatment plants, and not enough of the necessary chemicals are available to properly treat the water. This is in part because of restrictions in the supply of chlorine because of its weaponization by ISIS fighters.[91] Even if the chemicals were more readily available, the high salinity of the Shatt al-Arab makes the chemicals less effective in eliminating or neutralizing contamination in the water supply.[92]

Agriculture in the region has suffered as well and has served to contribute to problems such as salinization of the existing freshwater resources. Some of the challenges facing Iraqi farmers are due to the inadequate means of transporting water to fields. Because of this, water is often transported through earthen ditches and canals, resulting in a great deal of water being lost to evaporation and seepage.[93] In some cases, flood irrigation is still being used, which has the effect of drawing salts to the surface and rendering the soil infertile.

4.2.3 Deliberate Destruction

The deliberate draining of the marshes in the 1990s, by then Iraqi leader Saddam Hussein, was an ecological and humanitarian catastrophe that received comparatively little international attention. A 5,000 year-old culture was destroyed along with the 12,000 square miles of marshes they called home. The Ma'dan people of the marshes, known as Marsh Arabs, composed a number of Shi'a tribes.[94] Their estimated numbers in the 1950s were about 400,000. As recently as 1991 the population was estimated at 250,000.[95] Under Hussein, their population was decimated through forceful displacement, bombings, executions and the wholesale destruction of the marshes.[96] By 2003, only 40,000 Marsh Arabs remained in their original homeland.[97] Claiming that it was part of an agricultural improvement plan, the destruction was in actuality part of a larger campaign to repress the Shi'a population and retribution for participation in uprisings against the government. In the end, some estimates hold that the

90 L. Ali, 'In Basra: Oil in Abundance, but Little Water to Drink', UNICEF Connect Blog (16 July 2019), https://blogs.unicef.org/blog/basra-oil-abundance-little-water-drink/.

91 Belkis, *supra* note 78.

92 *Id.*

93 FAO in Iraq, 'Iraq at a Glance', (n.d.), http://www.fao.org/iraq/fao-in-iraq/iraq-at-a-glance/en/.

94 USIP, *supra* note 66.

95 Human Rights Watch, *The Iraqi Government Assault on the Marsh Arabs*, Briefing Paper (January 2003), https://www.hrw.org/legacy/backgrounder/mena/marsharabs1.htm.

96 *Id.*

97 USIP, *supra* note 66.

number of Marsh Arabs who were killed or displaced through this campaign at 170,000 to 190,000.[98] As part of this attack on the Marsh Arabs, the ecosystem of the marshes was destroyed. The army laid concealed mines in and around the river entrances to target those who were entering or leaving the area.[99] The marshes were burned and then drained by building dams and dikes to block water from entering them.

Following the end of Saddam Hussein's regime, the dams and dikes that prevented water from entering the marshes began to be dismantled. As water once again entered, the marshes began to spring to life again. By 2006 nearly 60% of the marshes that had been present in the 1970s had been restored along with a 'remarkable rate of reestablishment' of native species.[100] Since 2006, however, a number of factors, including upstream water developments, once again threaten the existence of this ecosystem.

4.2.4 Iran's Manipulation of Tributary Flows

In addition to the threats of lost water posed by the water projects on the Tigris and Euphrates, Iran has cut off or reduced flow to 42 tributaries to the Tigris.[101] Iran has built 109 dams on these tributaries and has completely changed the course of the Karun River. One Iraqi parliament member noted that this situation was far more dangerous than the issue of the dams.[102] The Tigris receives about 10% of its water from Iran's tributaries,[103] making this loss of flow a significant problem for Iraq.[104]

4.3 *Global Responsibility*

The Mesopotamian Marshes, recognized by UNESCO for their 'outstanding universal value,' wither and flourish in tandem with the quality of life and health of the Iraqi people. War, drought, corruption and mismanagement, and an international failure to engage in collaborative development, are the obstacles to restoration of the Mesopotamian Marshes and quality of life for the people of

---

98 J. F. Tanner, *The Internally Displaced People of Iraq* (The Brookings Institution, 2002), at 33.

99 USIP, *supra* note 66.

100 NASA, 'World of Change: Mesopotamia Marshes', Earth Observatory (n.d.), https://earthobservatory.nasa.gov/world-of-change/Iraq.

101 O. Sattar, *'Iraq Fears Bevy of Levees Will Mean Parched Years Ahead'*, *AL-Monitor* (5 April 2019).

102 *Id.*

103 FAO, AQUASTAT *Transboundary River Basin Overview—Euphrates-Tigris* (Rome: FAO, 2009).

104 T. Badawi, *'Iran's Upstream Hegemony and its Water Policies towards Iraq'*, Italian Institute for International Political Studies Commentary (26 February 2020), https://www.ispionline.it/en/pubblicazione/irans-upstream-hegemony-and-its-water-policies-towards-iraq-25173.

Iraq. To overcome these obstacles will take an international effort that reaches beyond the immediate stakeholders in the region's water resources. The effects of rendering an entire region uninhabitable will have global ramifications and can therefore only be addressed on a global scale.

5 Water Projects Affecting the Tigris Euphrates Basin

5.1 *Iraq*

Dependent on irrigation for its agriculture, the region that is now Iraq has a long history as the principal user of water from the Tigris and Euphrates Rivers dating back at least 6,000 years.[105] With the completion of the Hindiya barrage in 1913, Iraq also encompasses the region in which the first new waterworks on the rivers were constructed.[106] Since the beginning of human settlements in this region, the manipulation of the rivers has been necessary to avoid flood and to irrigate crops. These manipulations have almost always carried unintended consequences, complicating social and political matters and necessitating further developments to remedy the problems. In this respect, the construction of the Hindya barrage was no different.

Incapable of containing the spring rains, the Euphrates River was subject to severe flooding. In order to remedy this situation, the Saklawiya Canal, 'constructed in ancient days', connected the Euphrates and the Tigris just south of Baghdad.[107] Farther south, the Euphrates itself separated into two streams. The western arm was known as the Hindyia branch, and the eastern arm was known as the Hilla branch. The Hindya branch was the original riverbed of the Euphrates and flowed at a lower altitude than the artificial construction of the Hilla, which flowed through what was then known as Babylon and provided irrigation for the area.[108] Following the closure of the Saklawiya Canal in the late nineteenth century by Midhat Pasha, the Vali of Baghdad, the lower Hindyia branch could not sustain the increased flows, and the earthen dams that forced water into the higher elevation Hilla branch were washed away.[109] The Hilla began to silt up and a large agricultural area was threatened. To remedy the situation, the Turkish (Ottoman) government began a series of processes that, through a contract with a British company, resulted in the

105 Naff, *supra* note 37, at 89.

106 *Id.*

107 R. Money, '*The Hindiya Barrage, Mesopotamia*', 50(3) The Geographical Journal (1917) 217–222, at 217, www.jstor.org/stable/1779909, accessed 6 March 2020.

108 *Id.*

109 *Id.*

erection of a modern barrage at the Hindya branch. Work was completed in 1913 before war was declared and was still intact after the fall of Baghdad in 1917.[110]

Following Iraq's independence in 1932, population growth, urbanization and economic development led to an increased demand for water and spurred the building of more dams on both rivers. These included another barrage on the Euphrates in 1950, also for flood control and irrigation, as well as the construction of the Tharthar Canal, which links the Tigris and Euphrates and provides flood control on the Tigris. Development of these projects was in part driven by a fear of losing water due to upstream developments by Turkey and Syria.[111]

5.2 *Syria*

In terms of large dams, Syria's Tabqua High Dam or al-Tawtah Dam on the Euphrates was its first major project. After conducting research toward the end of the 1950s, the USSR proposed the dam at Tabqua. In 1966, through a Syrian–Soviet agreement, construction on the dam began and was completed in 1973.[112] Syria began to impound water behind the Tabqua in 1974–1975. Another project, the Bath Dam, completed in 1986, was not able to provide for as much hydropower or irrigation as the Tabqua.[113]

5.3 *Turkey*

In 1966, close to the time Syria was beginning construction on the Tabqua High Dam, Turkey began constructing the Keban Dam. Turkey also began to impound water behind the Keban in 1974, around the same time Syria was impounding water behind the Tabqua. This set of competing and uncoordinated manipulations of the Euphrates caused a significant decrease in the flow of water to Iraq, which in turn led to serious tensions between the neighbours and ultimately led both Syria and Iraq to move troops toward their borders.[114]

Turkey's initial drive to begin developing water projects on the Euphrates was an interest in the production of hydroelectric power.[115] In the 1980s, Turkey began development of its massive water project, the Greater Anatolia Project or 'GAP'. This project targeted the southeast Turkish portion of the TE Basin for the building of several dams to provide power and develop the agricultural

---

110 *Id.*

111 Kirschner & Tiroch, *supra* note 36, at 337.

112 J. de Onis, '*A Step into the 20th Century*', The New York Times (15 July 1973), at 173.

113 FAO, 'Euphrates Tigris: Water Development in the Basin', FAO Aquastat (2016), http://www.fao.org/NR/water/aquastat/countries_regions/profile_segments/euphrates.tigris-IrrDr_eng.stm.

114 Naff, *supra* note 37, at 93.

115 *Id.*

potential of the region. The GAP consists of 22 dams and 19 hydroelectric power stations on the Tigris and Euphrates. In 1992, the Ataturk Dam was completed, representing the largest project of the GAP. When Turkey began to fill the Ataturk, it once again sparked serious tensions among neighbours with both Syria and Iraq claiming that they were not given notice of the cut off in water supply. Turkey countered that it had given timely notice that the water supply of the Euphrates could be stopped for as much as a month.[116]

5.3.1 Turkey's Ilisu Dam

The Ilisu is the most recent GAP development on the Tigris, and the reservoir behind the dam is the largest on the Tigris.[117] The dam is one of the world's most controversial because of the ecological, cultural and human rights impacts it will have. The filling of the reservoir will not only further affect the downstream flows into an already water starved region, it has also inundated an area containing the 12,000 year old city of Hasankeyf, causing the destruction of one of the oldest continually occupied cities and resulting in the displacement of an estimated 80,000 people. There has also been irreversible ecological damage caused by the filling of the dam. For example, the banks of the Tigris behind the Ilisu Dam were home to some of the last remaining nesting areas for the nearly extinct Euphrates soft-shelled turtle.[118]

Construction of the Ilisu was first taken up in 1999.[119] Fearing the impact that the dam would have on their water resources, Iraq and Syria took the unusual step of appealing directly to European states protesting investments.[120] Within Turkey and throughout the West there was also strong opposition to the project. According to surveys, an estimated 80% of affected citizens were opposed to the dam.[121] Opposition to the project included heavy involvement of non-governmental organizations that are mainly concerned with the impacts the dam will have within Turkey.[122] In 2009, European banks withdrew funding after 'Turkish authorities repeatedly violated and failed to fulfil

116 Turkish Ministry of Foreign Affairs, *Water Issues Between Turkey, Syria, and Iraq* (n.d.).

117 Bremer, *supra* note 7.

118 P. Hockenos, '*Turkey's Dam Building Spree Continues, At Steep Ecological Cost*', Yale Environment 360 (3 October 2019), https://e360.yale.edu/features/turkeys-dam-building-spree-continues-at-steep-ecological-cost.

119 *Id.*

120 *Id.*

121 BankTrack, 'Ilisu Dam, Turkey', https://www.banktrack.org/project/ilisu_dam/pdf.

122 Bremer, *supra* note 7.

153 conditions attached to the guaranties',[123] and it became evident that Turkey could not comply with World Bank environmental and cultural preservation standards.[124] This marked the first time that funding for such a project was withdrawn on social and environmental grounds after approval.[125] In 2010, the European Parliament called for a cease to construction based on the consequences within Turkey, specifically the destruction of the archaeological sites of Hasankeyf and Allianoi and the 'displacement of thousands of people'.[126] That same year, Turkey secured enough new financing from three Turkish banks, Akbank, Garantibank and Halkbank, to make up for the shortfall. Even though the international community rejected funding for the Ilisu, it is notable that two of these Turkish banks are partially owned by American and Spanish banks.[127]

The dam was completed in February 2018. On 1 June 2018, Turkey began impounding water behind the Ilisu Dam. On 7 June Turkey announced that it would stop impoundment and that the gates were open and allowing all water to flow into the river. Turkey's Ambassador to Iraq, Fatih Yildiz, cited concerns over stability as the reason for the decision.[128] In May 2019, the European Court for Human Rights declined to hear a suit opposing the impoundment of water behind the Ilisu and inevitable destruction of Hasankeyf on the grounds that it lacked jurisdiction.[129] In August 2019, the Turkish government gave residents of Hasankeyf a deadline of 8 October 2019 to evacuate, stating that access and egress to the town would be closed.[130] When 8 October came the threat was

---

123 BankTrack, 'Ilisu Dam, Turkey: Financiers', https://www.banktrack.org/project/ilisu_dam#financiers, accessed 9 April 2020.

124 B. Walton, '*New Bank Loans Revive Controversial Ilisu Dam Project in Turkey*', Circle of Blue (13 January 2010), https://www.circleofblue.org/2010/world/new-bank-loans-revive-controversial-ilisu-dam-project-in-turkey/.

125 BankTrack (Financiers), *supra* note 123.

126 European Parliament, Parliament Resolution of 10 February 2010 on Turkey's progress report 2009, P7_TA(2010)0025, para. 16.

127 BankTrack (Financiers), *supra* note 123. BBVA of Spain owns about 24% of Garantibank, and Citibank of the United States owns about 20% of Akbank.

128 T. K. Aboulenein, '*Turkey Halts Filling Tigris Dam after Iraq Complains of Water Shortages*', Reuters (7 June 2018), https://www.reuters.com/article/us-iraq-turkey/turkey-halts-filling-of-ilisu-dam-until-july-ambassador-to-iraq-idUSKCN1J320X.

129 European Court of Human Rights (ECHR), 'An Application Concerning the Potential Impact of Construction of the Ilisu Dam on the Hasankeyf Archaeological Site: Inadmissible', Press Release ECHR 072 (2019) (21 February 2019).

130 B. Katz, '*Turkey is Moving Forward with Plans to Flood a 10,000 Year Old City*', Smithsonian Magazine (12 September 2019), https://www.smithsonianmag.com/smart-news/turkey-moving-forward-its-plans-flood-10000-year-old-city-180973124/.

not carried out.[131] On 9 October 2019, Turkey launched a ground and air assault on northern Syria.[132]

Supporters of the dam argue that Turkey's dependence on oil and other fossil fuels is what necessitates the dam and that it is hypocritical for Western critics to object to this project that holds the promise of greater energy independence.[133] Whether or not hydropower is the answer to this problem can be debated, however. According to a study by the European Climate Foundation, Turkey has a great deal of capacity in wind and solar energy potential that it could easily tap without a great deal of expense.[134]

The Iraq Ministry of Water Resources estimated in 2006 that the GAP irrigation schemes will reduce flow at the border by about 5.58 cubic kilometres or 34%.[135] For every cubic km of water lost, an area of 625 km^2 is no longer able to be farmed due to lost irrigation. This loss of water also accelerates desertification and is predicted to reduce energy production on the Mosul Dam by about 53%. Water quality will also be affected because return flows of agricultural runoff from irrigation will carry fertilizers and pesticides, further compromising the Iraqi drinking water supply. Turkey's environmental impact assessment report (EIAR) disputes these figures, finding that the irrigation scheme will withdraw only 1.91 km^3.[136] Numerous international organizations found the EIAR to be 'seriously flawed and in breach of internationally accepted practice'[137] calling into question the reliability of Turkey's assertion. Regardless of the reliability of these estimations, the hydroelectric power plant will require storage of water during the rainy season to use as flow during the dry season. This will change the natural flow of the river.[138] It is expected that there will be significant fluctuations during the course of any given day based on demand. In order to ameliorate these effects, the Cizre Dam is being built at the border to balance the fluctuations caused by the Ilisu.

131 A. Wilks, *'History Threatened as Turkey Prepares to Flood Ancient City'*, Aljazzera (7 October 2019).

132 B. G. Hubbard, *'Turkey Launches Offensive against U.S. Backed Syrian Militia'*, The New York Times (9 October 2019).

133 Hockenos, *supra* note 118.

134 P. E. Gordon, *Increasing the Share of Renewables in Turkey's Power System: Options for Transmission Expansion and Flexibility* (Istanbul: SHURA Energy Transition Center, 2018).

135 Bremer, *supra* note 7.

136 *Id.*

137 Ilisu Dam Campaign, *Review of EIAR for the Ilisu Dam and HEPP* (2001).

138 Bremer, *supra* note 7.

6 The Law

•••

> 'Have you also learned that secret from the river; that there is no such thing as time?' That the river is everywhere at the same time, at the source and at the mouth, at the waterfall, at the ferry, at the current, in the ocean and in the mountains, everywhere and that the present only exists for it, not the shadow of the past nor the shadow of the future.[139]

∴

The law of international watercourses, which has evolved over centuries, has been able to provide some measure of assistance in international conflict resolution and avoidance. Early development in this area was primarily focused on agreements around navigation, which contributed to the later development of the law of non-navigational uses.[140] Unlike navigational uses of a waterway, it is more difficult to address harm associated with a non-navigational use. 'It is often far less obvious that a non-navigational use will affect another state; such effects are frequently of an incremental, cumulative nature. This makes the effects difficult to deal with, since by the time they are felt in one state, the uses causing them may have become entrenched in the other state'.[141]

In addition, the nature of the hydrologic cycle, combined with rapid changes in climate and water use, have meant that the normally slow and incremental evolution of law has not been able to match the more rapid development of the conflicts it is meant to address.[142] Over the last few decades, conflicts, specifically armed conflicts, over water have increased worldwide.[143]

139 H. Hesse, *Siddhartha* (New York: New Directions, 1922, 1951).

140 McCaffrey (2007), *supra* note 25, at 57.

141 *Id.*, at 65.

142 *Id.*

143 Pacific Institute, 'Violence over Water Increases: New Data from Water Conflict Chronology', Announcement (5 November 2019), https://pacinst.org/announcement/violence-over-water-increases-new-data-from-the-water-conflict-chronology/#:~:text=November%205%2C%202019%2C%20Oakland%2C,accounts%2C%20and%20other%20conflict%20databases.

In some regions, for example, existing conflict, the political stance of leaders and other factors have proven the existing system of international law inadequate to provide protection of human and environmental water needs. This is the case with the TE Basin, and more specifically, the Tigris River. This section will first discuss the approach to the law of international watercourses taken by the various riparian countries of the Tigris River. Then the international agreements among states riparian to the Tigris will be discussed. Finally, norms of customary international law will be examined to determine how they may apply to this particular situation, and whether there are alternative approaches to increasing collaboration in the region.

As is often the case with disputes over transboundary waters, disagreement over the facts can be as much a problem as disagreement over obligations under international law. The facts surrounding how much water is available, who is causing the most pollution, who is using too much water and why, and whether one use is more valid than another, are often underlying the larger disagreement of who is entitled to what percentage of the water.

6.1 *Outdated and Inequitable Approaches to Resource Allocation*

Prior to the development of customary international law governing transboundary watercourses, two opposing approaches were employed by states in their claims to transboundary watercourses.[144]

The doctrine of absolute territorial sovereignty, also known as or closely identified with the Harmon Doctrine, which will be discussed at greater length below in this monograph, is named after an 1895 opinion written by U.S. Attorney General Judson Harmon regarding a dispute between Mexico and the United States over the waters of the Rio Grande.[145] It stands for the

144 UN Watercourses Convention, 'User's Guide Factsheet Series Number 10: Theories of Resource Allocation', https://www.unwatercoursesconvention.org/documents/UNWC-Fact-Sheet-10-Theories-of-Resource-Allocation.pdf, accessed 21 October 2020.

145 21 Op. U.S. Att'y Gen. (1898) 274, at 280. The Harmon Doctrine is the product of a dispute between two states over a shared watercourse in one of the more arid sections of the globe. The United States and Mexico share both the Colorado River and the Rio Grande. While it is a far less significant river in all respects than the Tigris, the Rio Grande holds a great deal of importance for the arid region encompassing northern Mexico and the southwestern United States. Because of the rapid and perhaps inappropriate development of agriculture in the southwestern United States during the late nineteenth and early twentieth centuries, numerous diversions of water from the Rio Grande had decreased the amount of water flowing into Mexico to the degree that the existence of its northern communities was threatened. Discussed at greater length in the following section, the Harmon Doctrine is essentially based on two paragraphs of an opinion written by then Attorney General Judson Harmon on the need for an agreement over how

principle that a State has the right to do with the waters within its borders as it wishes without regard for the impacts on neighbouring States. 'In short it insists upon the complete freedom of action of the upstream state'.[146] As a governing principle of international law, it has never been widely accepted and is 'at best an anachronism that has no place in today's interdependent, water-scarce world'.[147] Whether most states that assert this doctrine in their rhetoric actually follow through in practice is in question. Even in the resolution of the controversy that resulted in the Harmon Doctrine, a position of absolute sovereignty was not ultimately adopted.[148]

The conflicting doctrine of absolute territorial integrity is likewise disfavoured in that it forecloses development of an upstream state's resources by opposing any upstream development that might threaten the activities of the downstream state by reducing the amount of water it receives.[149] This theory is inequitable in that it prevents the upstream state from meeting its needs by essentially allocating the entire share of the watercourse to the downstream state.[150]

These approaches are inequitable in that they favour either the downstream or the upstream riparian state without regard for the consequences on the other of foreclosing use and development of the watercourse.[151] Both approaches lead to a fundamentally inequitable result, and neither is recognized to any meaningful extend in international law.[152] Although the doctrine of absolute territorial sovereignty is generally rejected along with its polar opposite, the doctrine of absolute territorial integrity, both seem to enjoy at least a symbolic embrace when questions of conflict, national sovereignty and competition over resources arise.

Turkey, in its approach, appears to give a nod to the doctrine of equitable and reasonable utilization while simultaneously adhering, to some extent, to the doctrine of absolute territorial sovereignty. In this case, Turkey is arguably

---

to equitably share the waters of the Rio Grande. The opinion cites a then eighty-year old case on sovereign immunity in asserting, fundamentally, that the sovereignty of a state includes the right to do what it will with the waters that happen to be momentarily within its borders without regard to the consequences to other downstream states.

146 UN Watercourses Convention Factsheet, *supra* note 145.

147 McCaffrey (2007), *supra* note 25, at 113.

148 *Id.*

149 UN Watercourses Convention Factsheet, *supra* note 144.

150 W. A. Qureshi, '*Equitable Apportionment of Shared Transboundary River Waters: A Case Study of Modifications of the Indus Waters Treaty*', 18 San Diego International Law Journal (2017) 199–240, at 205.

151 *Id.*, at 202–203.

152 *Id.*

acknowledging the needs of its neighbours while simultaneously asserting its control of the water as the upstream state.

A study by the Turkish Ministry of Foreign Affairs recognizes that water is now a primary problem in relations between Middle East countries, and that the current water resources in the Middle East have 'become insufficient to meet needs'.[153] Turkey, as the upstream state for much of the water flowing into Iraq and Syria, nonetheless maintains that it has no excess water capacity and that it too will be experiencing a water shortage in the near future.[154] The study refers to findings that the amount of water available per capita in Turkey is actually lower than that in Iraq and only marginally higher than in Syria with 1830, 2110, and 1420 cubic metres of water per year per capita respectively.[155] All three countries have substantially less water than a country that might be considered 'water rich'.[156] Turkey additionally argues that the lands in Syria and Iraq are less fertile, and that the criteria being used by Syria and Iraq to determine water need is too arbitrary to justify water cutbacks in Turkey.[157]

With respect to the Euphrates, Turkey claims that 88.7% of the water potential of the Euphrates Basin originates in Turkey while Iraq contributes none. This claim is juxtaposed with Iraq's demand for 43% of the flow.[158]

With respect to the Tigris, Turkey claims that its watershed is responsible for 51.9% of Tigris water while Iraq is responsible for the other 48.1%. In terms of consumption of water, Turkey claims that Iraq seeks to consume 92.5% of the water and Turkey only 14.1%. Without factoring in Syria's needs, this already exceeds 100%.[159]

With regard to Iraq and Syria's assertion that they have acquired rights relating to their ancestral uses of the waters of the Tigris and Euphrates, Turkey refers to Professor Stephen McCaffrey's discussion on the limitations of the use of acquired rights as a way of limiting upstream development.[160]

> A downstream State that was first to develop its water resources could not foreclose later development by an upstream State by demonstrating that

153 Turkish Ministry of Foreign Affairs, *Water: A Source of Conflict or Cooperation in the Middle East?*, http://www.mfa.gov.tr/data/DISPOLITIKA/WaterASourceofConflictofCoopintheMiddleEast.pdf, accessed 25 October 2020.

154 *Id.*

155 *Id.*

156 *Id.*

157 *Id.*

158 *Id.*

159 *Id.*

160 *Id.*

> the later development would cause it harm; under the doctrine of equitable utilisation, the fact that a downstream State was 'first to develop' (and thus had made prior uses that would be adversely affected by new upstream uses) would be merely one of a number of factors to be taken into consideration in arriving at an equitable allocation of the uses and benefits of the watercourse.[161]

In citing this discussion, however, Turkey fails to acknowledge that the most typical pattern of development on a watercourse is that the later development of upstream resources is done by a less developed state with fewer resources, and it is the wealthier and more capable downstream state that is opposing this development. Egypt's opposition to Ethiopia's Grand Ethiopian Renaissance Dam on the Blue Nile is a more typical example of a controversy over upstream development involving the theory of acquired rights (this controversy is discussed further below for the purpose of comparison). This is not the case with the Tigris. Turkey is in a far more stable position than either of its downstream neighbours in terms of politics, economics and security.

With respect to the use of the Ilisu Dam and its potential impact on its downstream neighbours, Turkey claims that the primary use of the dam will be the production of hydropower. However, there are conflicting statements and even conflicting sentences referencing its use. In May 2020, Turkish President Erdogan referred to its irrigation potential when he announced the launching of the first turbine on the dam. 'We will start operating one of six turbines of Ilisu Dam, one of the largest irrigation and energy projects in our country'.[162]

In couching aspects of its assertion of control over the water of the Tigris and the Euphrates in accepted doctrines of international law, Turkey basically claimed the right to utilize the waters within its borders regardless of potential downstream impacts, asserting that it has a superior right to those waters.

---

161 S. C. McCaffrey, 'The Law of International Watercourses: Some Recent Developments and Unanswered Questions', 17 *Denver Journal of International Law and Policy* (1989) 505–526, at 509.

162 A. Kucukgocmen, '*Turkey to Start Power Generation in Huge Tigris Dam Next Week, Erdogan Says*', Reuters (11 May 2020), https://www.reuters.com/article/us-turkey-dam/turkey-to-start-power-generation-in-huge-tigris-dam-next-week-erdogan-says-idUSKBN22N2L7. Another example of was found on the Republic of Turkey Ministry of Foreign Affairs Ilisu Dam information page contains the following statement: 'The Ilisu dam is not designed just for irrigation, only for power generation: The water passing through the turbines has to flow back into the riverbed'. The page has since been taken down. Ministry of Affairs, 'Ilisu Dam' (n.d.), http://www.mfa.gov.tr/ilisu-dam.en.mfa.

Currently unfettered by binding international law, Turkey continued to press forward without the onus of mitigating downstream effects.[163]

Iraq as the downstream user of the water is fundamentally at the mercy of Syria and Turkey for its allotment of water from the rivers. This places it in the position of having to defend its water supply not only against the upstream use of the water for irrigation and power generation, but also the potential use of the water by upstream states as a political tool. Iraq maintains the position that its historic use of the water resulted in acquired rights that must not be interfered with by new upstream developments, essentially embracing the theory of absolute territorial integrity.[164]

Neither Iraq's nor Turkey's stance is supported to any extent by international water law. Neither stance recognizes that there are duties as well as rights with regard to the utilization of shared watercourses.[165] Given what is understood about the nature of the hydrologic cycle, not to mention the obvious consequences to neighbours of the pollution or overuse of a shared watercourse, such positions are politically dysfunctional.

6.2 *Limited Territorial Sovereignty and the Community of Interests*

Under the theory of limited territorial sovereignty, a state's sovereignty over the water within its borders is limited, essentially, by the duty not to harm its neighbours. This is reflected in Principle 2 of the Rio Declaration on Environment and Development, which reads:

> States have, in accordance with the Charter of the United Nations and the Principles of International Law, the sovereign right to exploit their own resources pursuant to their own environmental and developmental policies, and the responsibility to ensure that activities within their jurisdiction or control do not cause damage to the environment of other States or of areas beyond the limits of national jurisdiction.[166]

The Rio Declaration reflects a basic notion of 'good neighbourliness' without threatening to undermine notions of sovereignty. The potential arguments

163 Hockenos, *supra* note 118.

164 O. Ünver & A. Kibaroglu, '*An Institutional Framework for Facilitating Cooperation in the Euphrates-Tigris River Basin*', 5(2) International Negotiations (2000) 311–330. Accessed through ResearchGate, article paginated 1–24.

165 UN Watercourses Convention Factsheet, *supra* note 144.

166 United Nations Conference on the Environment and Development, *Rio Declaration on Environment and Development*, UN Doc A/CONF.151/26/Rev.1 (Vol. I) (12 August 1992), Annex I.

surrounding the terms 'cause' and 'damage' are where the ambiguity in this theory can begin to fester and infect the otherwise clear practicality of the theory. The doctrine of equitable and reasonable utilization of a watercourse will be explored below along with its capacity for ambiguity. Turkey argues that its use of the dam will not harm Iraq, that the water issues in Iraq are caused by a combination of climatic and social factors, and that the dam is meant to be a 'run of the river' dam that will not decrease the flow of the Tigris. That begs the question, however, of when, in the context of a changing climate and the needs of a growing population, a state must step away from the exploitation of resources to which it would otherwise be entitled.

The theory of a 'community of interests' pushes even further, past the zone of good neighbourliness, and into the zone of partnership and collaboration. Described in the *River Oder Case*, '[t]his community of interest in a navigable river becomes the basis of a common legal right, the essential features of which are the perfect equality of all riparian States in the user of the whole course of the river and the exclusion of any preferential privilege of any one riparian State in relation to the others'.[167] This principle was expanded later to apply to non-navigational uses of a transboundary water course by the International Court of Justice (ICJ) in the 1997 *Gabčíkovo-Nagymaros Case.* 'Modern development of international law has strengthened this principle for non-navigational uses of international watercourses as well'.[168] Given that Turkey, Iraq and Syria continue to adhere to the opposing approaches of absolute territorial sovereignty and absolute territorial integrity, they seem to be a long way from developing a Basin-wide regime based on a community of interests. This, however, is what may be required to establish a truly cooperative if not collaborative and sustainable regime.

6.3 *International Agreements Affecting the Tigris*

While water-related conflict in the TE Basin has been a recurring issue for thousands of years, there have been periods of relative tranquillity regarding the use of the rivers.[169] It was the onset of major developments on the rivers beginning in the late 1960s that spurred the signing of a number of protocols on the management of specific projects, as well as attempts to develop a basin-wide

167 *Case Relating to the Territorial Jurisdiction of the International Commission of the River Oder (United Kingdom v. Poland)*, Judgment No. 16, 1929 PCIJ (ser. A) No. 23 (September 10), para. 74.

168 *Gabčíkovo-Nagymaros Project (Hungary/Slovakia)*, Judgment, ICJ Reports 1997, p. 7, para. 85.

169 Ünver & Kibaroglu, *supra* note 164, at 2.

accord on the management of the Basin's water.[170] Such an accord has never been achieved, however, leaving the completion of projects such as the Ilisu Dam largely unfettered by binding agreements.

The establishment of agriculture in arid regions has, from the beginning, been a subject of both law and war. Some of the earliest records of human civilization tell us that the water supply of the TE Basin has been a source of conflict. The Louvre museum in Paris houses one of the first known records of a treaty on the sharing of transboundary water resources.[171] The Mesopotamian city states of Lagash and Umma went to war 4,500 years ago after Umma's king drained an irrigation canal leading from the Tigris.[172] Sixty people were killed in that battle.[173] This was possibly the world's first water war, and it resulted in one of the earliest treaties.

6.3.1 Colonial Era Agreements

For several hundred years, until the beginning of the twentieth century, the TE Basin was under the unified rule of the Ottoman Empire. For a time, the availability of water in the basin was a source of power for the Empire. As misuse of the rivers and other factors began to destabilize the region, this source of power became a liability.[174] The current state boundaries are a result of a hasty redrawing of the map following World War I.[175] The area was divided between three states, France, the United Kingdom and Turkey. The TE riparian countries were divided as follows: Iraq was left under the influence of the United Kingdom and Syria under that of France. The remainder became Turkey.[176] The manner in which these borders were drawn has since contributed to the region's instability in part because tribal lines were ignored during the process.[177]

---

170 *Id.*, at 3.

171 P. H. Sand, '*Mesopotamia 2550 B.C.: The Earliest Boundary Water Treaty*', 5(4) Global Journal of Archaeology and Anthropology (2018).

172 McCaffrey (2007), *supra* note 25, at 60.

173 J. Hammer, '*Is a Lack of Water to Blame for the Conflict in Syria?*' Smithsonian Magazine (June 2013), https://www.smithsonianmag.com/innovation/is-a-lack-of-water-to-blame-for-the-conflict-in-syria-72513729/.

174 F. H. Husain, 'The Tigris-Euphrates Basin under Early Modern Ottoman Rule, c. 1534–1830' (Ph.D. dissertation, Georgetown University, 2018), https://repository.library.georgetown.edu/handle/10822/1050792.

175 T. Osman, '*Why Borderlines Drawn with a Ruler, in WWI Still Rock the Middle East*', BBC News (14 December 2013), https://www.bbc.com/news/world-middle-east-25299553.

176 Treaty of Lausanne (Convention Respecting the Regime of the Straits and Instruments signed at Lausanne), signed 24 July 1923, 28 LNTS 11.

177 Osman, *supra* note 175.

A number of agreements were made between the colonial powers and Turkey that provided scanty coverage of the potential for conflict over the waters of the Tigris and Euphrates. Article 109 of the Treaty of Lausanne provides:

> In default of any provisions to the contrary, when as the result of the fixing of a new frontier the hydraulic system (canalization, inundation, irrigation, drainage or similar matters) in a state is dependent on works executed within the territory of another State, or when use is made on the territory of a State, in virtue of pre-war usage, of water or hydraulic power, the source of which is on the territory of another State, an agreement shall be made between the States concerned to safeguard the interests and rights acquired by each of them. Failing an agreement, the matter shall be regulated by arbitration.[178]

This brief reference to the arbitration of disputes over water rights has not become the basis for future agreements between Turkey and its post-colonial neighbours. It seems to be less an instruction as to how water should be shared and rather a provision for arbitration in the event the parties fail to agree.

Article 2 of the 1930 Final Protocol of the Commission on the Delimitation of the Turkish-Syrian Frontier specifies that all issues concerning the Tigris be determined on the basis of complete equality.[179] While none of these agreements laid out the foundations for multilateral treaties governing the use of the Tigris, there is among them some mention of equitable utilization of the rivers.

6.3.2 Post-World War II Agreements

On 23 March 1946, following the independence of Iraq and Syria, Iraq and Turkey signed the Treaty of Friendship and Neighbourly Relations.[180] This treaty contained six protocols, the first of which was 'relative to the regulation of the waters of the Tigris and Euphrates and of their tributaries'.[181] Protocol No. 1 essentially established a system through which Iraq and Turkey would collaborate in creating waterworks on the Tigris and Euphrates. 'Recognizing the importance for Iraq of the construction of conservation works on the Tigris and Euphrates and their tributaries, in order to ensure the maintenance of the two rivers with a view to avoiding the danger of floods during the annual

178 Treaty of Lausanne, *supra* note 176.

179 Kirschner & Tiroch, *supra* note 36.

180 Treaty of Friendship and Neighbourly Relations between Iraq and Turkey, signed 29 March 1946, 37 UNTS 226.

181 *Id.*, Protocol No. 1: Relative to the regulation of the waters of the Tigris and Euphrates and of their tributaries.

periods of high-water',[182] Protocol No. 1 went on to establish the likelihood that these works should most likely be built in Turkey and that the cost would be defrayed by Iraq.[183] Provisions for collaboration among the two countries' experts, observation stations in Turkey, and the requirement of frequent communication about conditions, as well as notification about plans for construction, provided a promising framework for a comprehensive water sharing regime. Protocol No. 1 was never implemented, however, and fell into disuse.[184]

One can only speculate how the application of Protocol No. 1 to the controversy over the Ilisu Dam, especially the requirement that 'Turkey shall keep Iraq informed of her plans for the construction of conservation works on either of the two rivers or their tributaries, in order that these works may as far as possible, be adapted, by common agreement, to the interests of both Iraq and Turkey',[185] may have altered the outcome. Would there be a firm commitment to use the dam for hydropower only, thereby theoretically resolving the problem of decreased flow? Would the countries agree to collaborate in devising mutually beneficial solutions? Nearly 80 years later the political climate in the region has change to such a degree that it is difficult to predict how Protocol No. 1 would be applied.

According to UN Water, since 1948 there have been 37 incidents of acute conflict over water and approximately 295 international agreements regarding water.[186] Even though other regions have managed to develop such agreements, there is little in the way of treaty agreement as to the sharing of the waters of the Tigris.

The increased use of the rivers by Turkey and Syria over the following decades, and the failure of the three countries to consult and cooperate (much less collaborate) on water projects, led to a number of crises. For example, in 1975, unilateral development on the Euphrates of Syria's Tabqa Dam and Turkey's Keban Dam nearly brought the three riparian states to the brink of warfare.[187] Iraq blamed the Syrians for a sharp decrease in flow, and the Syrians claimed it was due to reduced flows from Turkey.[188] Only the intervention of

182 *Id.*, preambular para. 1.

183 *Id.*, Articles 1, 3.

184 Kirschner & Tiroch, *supra* note 36.

185 Protocol No. 1, *supra* 182, Article 5.

186 UN Water, 'Transboundary Waters: Facts and Figures', https://www.unwater.org/water-facts/transboundary-waters/.

187 A. Wolf, *Middle East Water Conflicts and Directions for Conflict Resolution* (Washington, D.C.: International Food Policy Research Center, 1996), at 7.

188 *Id.*, at 8.

Saudi Arabia was able to bring the three parties to an agreement, the terms of which were never made public.[189]

The GAP developments beginning in the 1980s spurred more attempts to cooperate over the use of water in the region. The Joint Technical Committee for Regional Waters was established in 1983 to manage all issues related to water between the TE Basin riparian states in compliance with international law.[190] After 16 meetings talks reached an impasse that related to disagreements about 'both the subject and the object of negotiations: whether the Euphrates and the Tigris could be considered a single water system, or whether the discussions should be limited to the Euphrates'.[191] Turkey held the view that the Tigris and Euphrates should be considered as a whole system, thereby theoretically making available water from the Tigris in the event of a shortfall from the Euphrates. Iraq and Syria insisted that only the Euphrates should be considered out of fear that the added flexibility of a Basin approach might result in even further reductions in the flow of the Euphrates.[192] These differences, based on the parties' motivation to maximize their own beneficial uses of the Euphrates, undermined any potential foundation for collaboration. The Committee broke apart in 1993 without accomplishing anything.[193]

In 1984 Turkey proposed 'the most comprehensive water management plan brought forward by one of the riparian states',[194] the 'Three-Staged Plan for Optimum, Equitable, and Reasonable Utilisation of the Trans-boundary Watercourses of the Euphrates-Tigris Basin'.[195] Stage 1 would be an inventory of water resources involving the exchange of available data on levels and discharges from select gauging stations. 'Experts from the three countries would agree upon the nomination of representative meteorological stations in the TE basin and exchange data about them as well as all available data from them concerning evaporation, temperature, rainfall, and snowfall (if available) on a monthly basis'. Stage 2 would entail an inventory study of land resources, including, among other things, the exchange of information concerning soil classification methods and drainage criteria practiced in each country, and the

189 Naff, *supra* note 38.

190 FAO Aquastat, *supra* note 4.

191 Ünver & Kibaroglu, *supra* note 164, at 2.

192 *Id.*, at 321.

193 FAO Aquastat, *supra* note 4.

194 Kirschner & Tiroch, *supra* note 36, at 385.

195 Turkish Ministry of Foreign Affairs, *Water Issues Between Turkey, Syria, and Iraq*. Since first retrieving this information, the webpage has been replaced by another with largely similar information. See Turkish Ministry of Foreign Affairs, *Water: A Source of Conflict of Cooperation in the Middle East?*, *supra* note 154.

checking of soil conditions for projects that are planned, under construction, or in operation. Stage 3 would be an evaluation of water and land resources involving, among other things, a discussion of methods and criteria for determining the economic viability of the planned projects.[196] The plan adheres to the principal of equitable utilization[197] in that calls for the joint gathering and assessment of data and the evaluation of not just water quantity but a 'broad analysis of water and land resources encompassing both strategies on resource as well as demand management'.[198] This, in theory, would lay the groundwork for genuine cooperation among the three states that could lead to the equitable utilization of the rivers. The plan is based on the recognition of the TE Basin as a single system rather than two separate ones, and therein lie at least part of the grounds for objection on the part of Syria and Iraq. The two countries also argued that the plan infringed on their sovereignty, and Iraq was concerned that Turkey might, through the use of the inventory studies, make an issue of inefficiencies in its agricultural practices.[199]

In 1987, a few years ahead of the filling of the Ataturk Dam, Turkey and Syria signed the Protocol on Matters Pertaining to Economic Cooperation. As part of this agreement, Turkey was to let an average of 500 cubic metres per second of water through to Syria.[200] Later, in 1990, the Syrian Arab Republic entered into an agreement with Iraq to share the allocation of water from Turkey, with Iraq receiving 58% and Syria 42%.[201] In 1992 the Ataturk Dam was completed. Its filling stopped the flow of the Euphrates for a period of a month, which led to conflict with Syria and Iraq. In 2008, Turkey, Syria and Iraq agreed to establish a Water Institute comprised of water experts from each state that would be tasked with working out solutions to water-related problems among the TE Basin riparians.[202]

Outside of a number of memoranda of understanding (MOU) signed in 2009, the three states, to this day, do not have a formal agreement as to the use of either Euphrates or Tigris water. These MOUs include consideration

196 *Id.*

197 FAO Aquastat, *supra* note 4.

198 Kirschner & Tiroch, *supra* note 36, at 385.

199 *Id.*, at 384–385.

200 Protocol on matters pertaining to economic cooperation between the Syrian Arab Republic and the Republic of Turkey, signed and in force 17 July 1987, 1724 UNTS 3 (1993). Article 6 provides: 'During the filling up period of the Ataturk Dam reservoir and until final allocation of the waters of the Euphrates among the three riparian countries, the Turkish Side undertakes to release a yearly average of more than 500 M^3/Sec., five hundred cubic meter per second at the Turkish-Syrian Borders'.

201 FAO Aquastat, *supra* note 4.

202 *Id.*

of issues of sustainability, such as drought mitigation, preservation of water resources and water in both quantity as well as quality, and represent promising steps in the direction of cooperation. The need for a trilateral agreement remains, however, and increased consideration of environmental protection will be necessary if resources such as the Mesopotamian Marshes are to be restored and protected.

6.3.3 The Helsinki Rules

The International Law Association (ILA) is an international, non-governmental organization founded in 1873 with the objective of 'the study, clarification and development of international law, both public and private, and the furtherance of international understanding and respect for international law'.[203] In 1966 the ILA adopted the Helsinki Rules on the Uses of the Waters of International Rivers.[204] In 2004 the Helsinki Rules were updated to reflect the 'present state of customary international water law'.[205] The revised rules, known as the Berlin Rules, 'embraced and expounded the principle of reasonable and equitable utilization'.[206] Although this important contribution to the law of international watercourses is not binding international law, the Helsinki Rules are widely known and hold significant authority.[207] Chapter Two, Article IV of the Helsinki Rules lays out the principle of equitable utilization of the waters of an international drainage basin: 'Each basin state is entitled, within its territory, to a reasonable and equitable share in the beneficial uses of the waters of an international drainage basin'. Chapter 2, Article V states that the determination of reasonableness is to be made in light of all the relevant factors in each case and provides a non-exclusive list of eleven such factors:

1. The geography of the basin, including in particular the extent of the drainage area in the territory of each basin state
2. The hydrology of the basin, including in particular the contribution of water by each basin state
3. The climate affecting the basin

---

203 International Law Association (ILA), 'About Us,' https://www.ila-hq.org/index.php/about-us, accessed 12 September 2020.

204 ILA, *Report of the Fifty-second Conference, Helsinki* (London: ILA, 1966), 447–533 [Helsinki Rules].

205 S. M. A. Salman, '*The Helsinki Rules, the UN Watercourses Convention and the Berlin Rules: Perspectives on International Water Law*', 23(4) International Journal of Water Resources Development (2007) 625–640, at 631.

206 *Id.*

207 McCaffrey (2007), *supra* note 25, at 535, footnote 1.

4. The past utilization of the waters of the basin, including in particular existing utilization
5. The economic and social needs of each basin state
6. The population dependent on the waters of the basin in each basin State
7. The comparative costs of alternative means of satisfying the economic and social needs of each basin state
8. The availability of other resources
9. The avoidance of unnecessary waste in the utilization of waters of the basin
10. The practicability of compensation to one or more of the co-basin States as a means of adjusting conflicts among uses
11. The degree to which the needs of a basin State may be satisfied, without causing substantial injury to a co-basin State.

Some of these factors are at issue in the factual disagreements between Turkey and Iraq. For example, the ninth factor, the avoidance of unnecessary waste in the utilization of waters of the basin, is directly relevant to Turkey's claim that Iraq's water shortages are in part due to its wasteful use of the water. It also speaks to an underlying reason for Iraq's rejection of Turkey's Three Stage Plan, namely that Turkey would expose and utilize Iraq's inefficiencies against it in determining water allocation.[208] Whether Iraq's use is wasteful is a matter of fact that also must be considered in light of the ongoing war and political instability in the country. While Turkey has had the opportunity to develop its water infrastructure, Iraq's has been destroyed along with its ability to efficiently use water. It has been proposed that water might be most efficiently stored in Turkish reservoirs for release as needed to Syria and Iraq, thereby avoiding loss by evaporation in the more arid region.[209] That proposition may also relate to the seventh factor in that it suggests an alternative means for Iraq to have access to the water without maintaining the natural flow of the river.

6.3.4 The UN Watercourses Convention

On 21 May 1997 the United Nations General Assembly adopted the Convention on the Law of the Non-Navigational Uses of International Watercourses (UN Watercourses Convention).[210] This Convention represents the only universally applicable framework establishing rules for the sharing and protection

208 Kirschner & Tiroch, *supra* note 36, at 385.

209 Ohara et al., *supra* note 34; Brown, *supra* note 49; Roston & Bloomberg, *supra* note 49.

210 Convention on the Law of the Non-navigational Uses of International Watercourses, adopted 21 May 1997, in force 17 August 2014, 2999 UNTS [UN Watercourses Convention].

of international watercourses.[211] A codification of the existing fundamental norms and obligations of international water law, it was passed by an overwhelming margin, 103 adopting, 3 opposing, and the rest either absent or abstaining. The Convention held a great deal of promise as a mechanism for ensuring the 'utilization, development, conservation, management and protection of international watercourses and the promotion of the optimal and sustainable utilization thereof for present and future generations'[212] while 'affirming the importance of international cooperation and good neighborliness in the field'.[213] Both Iraq and Syria were among the 103 states that adopted the Convention. The three states opposing it were Burundi, China and Turkey.[214] Seventeen years later, in 2014, the Convention entered into force with only 36 ratifying parties.[215]

The Convention is composed of seven parts containing 37 articles. Parts II and III set out the substantive and procedural obligations in a partial reiteration of existing norms and authority. The foundational principle of 'equitable and reasonable utilization and participation' is set out in Part II, Article 5, with its defining components described in two paragraphs. Paragraph 1 of Article 5 establishes that 'an international watercourse shall be used and developed by watercourse States with a view to attaining optimal and sustainable utilization thereof and benefits therefrom, taking into account the interests of the watercourse states concerned, consistent with adequate protection of the watercourse'.

Paragraph 2 of Article 5 also defines the requirement of 'participation', providing a mandate that the 'Watercourse States shall participate in the use, development and protection of an international watercourse and try to cooperate in an equitable and reasonable manner', which includes 'both the right to utilize the watercourse and the duty to cooperate in the protection and development thereof'. This, finally, codifies the reality that 'a regime of equitable utilization of an international watercourse system, together with the protection and preservation of its ecosystems, cannot be achieved solely through

211 Kirschner & Tiroch, *supra* note 36, at 353.

212 UN Watercourses Convention, *supra* note 210.

213 Id.

214 United Nations General Assembly (UNGA), Press Release GA/9248, 99th Meeting (AM) 21 May 1997, https://www.internationalwaterlaw.org/documents/intldocs/convention_press.html.

215 International Water Law Project, 'Status of the Watercourses Convention as of 1 January 2020', https://www.internationalwaterlaw.org/documents/intldocs/watercourse_status.html.

individual action by each riparian state acting in isolation; again, affirmative cooperation will be necessary'.[216]

Article 6 sets forth a non-exclusive list of seven factors to be considered in the determination of whether a use is equitable and reasonable. The first on the list, factor (a), essentially includes the first three factors of the Helsinki Rules, namely the 'geographic, hydrographic, hydrological, climactic, ecological and other factors of a natural character'. The remaining six factors are as follows:

b. The social and economic needs of the watercourse states concerned
c. The population dependent on the watercourse in each watercourse state
d. The effects of the use or uses of the watercourse in one watercourse state on other watercourse states
e. The existing and potential uses of the watercourse
f. Conservation, protection, development and economy of use of the water resources of the watercourse and the costs of measures taken to that effect
g. The availability of alternatives, of comparable value, to a planned or existing use

Article 7 is one of the more controversial in that it addresses head on the inevitable occurrence of irreconcilable interests in the sharing of a watercourse. The wording of the two paragraphs of Article 7 introduces the possibility for accommodation of some harm.[217] Paragraph 1 requires that states shall 'take all appropriate measures to prevent the causing of significant harm to other watercourse States.' Paragraph 2, in providing for the case where 'significant harm nevertheless is caused to another watercourse State' requires that the 'State whose use causes such harm shall, in the absence of agreement to such use, take all appropriate measures, having due regard for the provisions of articles 5 and 6, in consultation with the affected State, to eliminate or mitigate such harm and, where appropriate, to discuss the question of compensation'. The terms 'appropriate' and 'significant' could be seen as equivocal and the requirement merely to 'discuss' the question of compensation may not provide the necessary incentive to persuade a state to forego activities of any 'significant' value.

Article 8, paragraph 1, establishes the obligation to cooperate 'on the basis of sovereign equality, territorial integrity, mutual benefit and good faith in order to attain optimal utilization and adequate protection of an international

216 S. C. McCaffrey, 'The Contribution of the UN Convention on the Law of the Non-Navigational Uses of International Watercourses', 1(3–4) *International Journal for Global Environmental Issues* (2001) 250–263, at 253.

217 *Id.*, at 255.

watercourse'. Paragraph 2 suggests possible mechanisms through which the states may cooperate. It is partly the lack of these mechanisms that has posed a barrier to the development of a binding trilateral agreement for the TE Basin.[218] Article 9 obligates states to exchange readily available data, comply with requests for data and use best efforts to collect data. These obligations would be largely dependent on the establishment of the mechanisms suggested in Article 8, paragraph 2.

These substantive provisions of the Convention, particularly those regarding cooperation, are inextricable from the procedural requirements of Part III, specifically Articles 11 and 12. Article 11 establishes the requirement to exchange information and consult, and 'if necessary, negotiate on the possible effects of planned measures'. Article 12 establishes a notification requirement: 'Before a watercourse State implements or permits the implementation of planned measures which may have a significant adverse effect upon other watercourse States, it shall provide those States with timely notification thereof'.

6.3.4.1 *The Ilisu Dam in Light of the Convention*

Turkey's refusal to sign on to the UN Watercourses Convention begs for an analysis of the degree to which the Convention has encompassed and codified already existing fundamental norms and obligations. International law derives from a number of sources, including customary law or those 'norms derived from the actual practice of States undertaken by these States in the belief that such practices are required by international law'.[219] It is often the case that a multilateral treaty may have the effect of 'induc(ing) states to consider that acting in a particular way is legally required'.[220] Such treaties may be considered by states to be a codification of preexisting international law.[221] The relationship of the Convention to existing customary international law is an important consideration in this context.

Even though Turkey had objected to the Convention, it has over time made reference to its compliance with some of the norms and obligations therein codified.[222] Therefore it has not objected to these norms as consistently as might be required so as not to be bound by them. Given the absence of any

218 Ünver & Kibaroglu, *supra* note 164, at 13.

219 E. Brown Weiss et al., *International Environmental Law and Policy* (Gaithersburg, MD: Aspen Law & Business, 1998), at 1275.

220 *Id.*, at 1276.

221 *Id.*

222 Publication by the Turkish Ministry of Foreign Affairs on Turkey's policy on Water Issues stating that:
- Turkey considers water as a source of cooperation among riparian countries.

international agreement governing the TE Basin, one may nonetheless look to these fundamental norms and obligations in the law of international watercourses for guidance on the legal obligations held by Turkey, Syria and Iraq with respect to sharing the waters of the TE Basin.

Evaluating the facts in light of the factors relevant to determining whether the building and filling of the Ilisu Dam adheres to the requirement of equitable and reasonable utilization is a field ripe for controversy. Studies analysing the potential for a comprehensive framework for governing the TE Basin point to a lack of trust, the absence of 'regularized institutions' and political tension as barriers to progress.[223] Without some level of transparent cooperation it will be difficult for the parties to come to agreement on the factors relevant to equitable and reasonable utilization. Factor (f), for example, refers to the economy of use of the watercourse. Would a state whose water infrastructure has been destroyed by warfare be less entitled to a share of water because it is unable to properly conserve the resource? What does Turkey's claim that it has seven times more irrigable land than Syria and that Iraq and Syria simply want to divert water away from fertile land and into areas of 'high salt and gypsum concentrations' mean in light of the Convention?[224] The devastation of the Mesopotamian Marshes is due to a variety of problems, all of which are arguably human made. Drought exacerbated by climate change, past acts of war, inefficient agricultural practices and the damming of the Tigris and the Euphrates and their tributaries are all contributing to their destruction. Turkey argues that the Ilisu will be used primarily for hydropower although there is also reference to irrigation. Would the drop in water caused by Turkey's filling of the dam place it in a position of having to comply with the requirement of Article 7(2) to mitigate the harm? Would not then all other perpetrators be obligated to provide such mitigation?

- Transboundary river basins have their own characteristics and peculiarities and each case of the transboundary waters reflects specific regional, economic, social, cultural, and historic aspects. Therefore, transboundary water issues should be addressed only among the riparian countries without interventions by third parties.
- Each riparian state of a transboundary river system has the sovereign right to make use of the water in its territory without giving 'significant harm' to other riparian countries.
- Transboundary waters should be used in an equitable, reasonable and optimum manner.

http://www.mfa.gov.tr/turkey_s-policy-on-water-issues.en.mfa, accessed 10 December 2020.

223 Ünver & Kibaroglu, *supra* note 164; see also Kirschner & Tiroch, *supra* note 36.

224 Turkish Ministry of Foreign Affairs, *Water: A Source of Conflict of Cooperation in the Middle East?*, *supra* note 154.

6.4 *Fundamental Norms and Obligations*

6.4.1 Equitable and Reasonable Utilization of an International Watercourse

The doctrine of equitable and reasonable utilization is recognized as the overarching principle governing the sharing of international watercourses.[225] While each state has a legal interest in an equitable share of the watercourse, it must also not infringe upon the rights of other states. 'According to the doctrine of equitable utilization, each state has a legally protected interest in an equitable share of the uses and benefits of an international watercourse'.[226] It is this legally protected interest that is protected from harm by this doctrine.[227] Neither geographic nor temporal priority is protected by the doctrine making it, in essence, antithetical to both the 'absolute territorial sovereignty' and 'absolute territorial integrity' theories of transboundary watercourses.[228] This legally protected interest is capable of changing as the share of water changes. Equitable does not mean equal, it is an inherently flexible standard capable of changing to meet changing circumstances. Reasonableness is also a requirement and, although there is little in the way of international jurisprudence to determine what might be unreasonable,[229] one wonders if the factors provided by the Helsinki Rules might be a guide. Reasonableness in that case would also be a matter to be measured against the circumstances.

Turkey and Iraq's contradicting positions on the relative amounts of water in each state, as well as the reasonableness of the use and manner of application of the water, represent the factual labyrinth to which the employment of a flexible standard of equitability and reasonableness can lead. It would be impossible to have a rigid system that could fairly allocate a resource whose presence and form is capable of changing as rapidly as water. However, there must also be some system by which the allocation of a resource so fundamentally necessary to all life can be more rapidly determined so that lives are not lost and ecosystems are not destroyed.

6.4.2 The Obligation to Prevent Harm to Other Riparian States

Also known as the no-harm rule, the obligation to prevent harm to other riparian states is another fundamental principle under international water law. This principle has been considered in a manner that is complementary to the

225 McCaffrey (2007), *supra* note 25, at 385.

226 *Id.*, at 388–389.

227 *Id.*

228 *Id.*, at 386.

229 *Id.*, at 389.

principle of equitable and reasonable use of a shared resource in that, rather than superseding the principle, it can facilitate negotiation on the prevention of specific harms.[230] The type of harm to be avoided is significant harm to either the quantity or quality of the water that is 'transmitted by means of an international watercourse'.[231] The prohibition is not absolute, it is a requirement that a state exercise due diligence and the prohibited harm must be 'significant'. While the case of an upstream state engaging in an activity that causes harm to a downstream state is the most obvious scenario, there is also the possibility of a downstream state using the water in a manner that threatens to legally foreclose the upstream state's ability to an equitable share of the water.[232]

In the case of the effect of the Ilisu Dam on the Mesopotamian Marshes, it is clearly the former and more obvious scenario that is in play. The factual questions again are at the heart of the disagreement. Is it Turkey's impact on the rivers that is causing harm or is it any one of the other impingements, such as Iran's interference with the tributaries or factors related to Iraq's use of the water? The ongoing and future effects of climate change are already a circumstance that must be considered.

6.4.3 The Obligation to Protect the Ecosystems on International Watercourses

While the obligation of states to protect the ecosystem of international watercourses may be considered to be 'emerging', its foundations are already part of international law.[233] The protection of the ecosystem of an international watercourse is in some way subsumed within the obligation of reasonable and equitable use. Those standards, however, are more anthropocentric in the definition of harm. The ecosystem of the Tigris would naturally include the Mesopotamian Marshes and a reduction in the flow of water would contribute to their destruction.

6.4.4 Procedural Obligations

In addition to the substantive obligations discussed above are the procedural obligations to notify, consult and cooperate. No less binding, the procedural obligations are in fact the roadmap to determining how the substantive

---

230 *Id.*, at 408.
231 *Id.*, at 409.
232 *Id.*, at 410.
233 *Id.*, at 461.

obligations can be met under a potentially infinite and constantly changing set of facts.[234]

The general obligation to cooperate is set forth in Part II, Article 8 of the UN Watercourses Convention. Whether this obligation is substantive or procedural, it is both a prerequisite and an objective of each of the other substantive and procedural obligations. Cooperation among states may seem to be the most logical and fundamental underpinning of any effort to sustainably develop and protect a shared resource. It is 'also an essential basis for the proper functioning of other procedural rules and for the attainment and maintenance of an equitable allocation of the uses and benefit of an international watercourse'.[235] As logical as its relationship to any of the more substantive obligations may be, its definition remains amorphous. Because cooperation is so essential to the successful execution of substantive obligations, its existence may be more recognizable in the acts taken or omissions made that would constitute its violation.[236] Its inclusion in the Convention, one of several different instruments to recognize its importance, constitutes a codification of a widely held understanding of the importance of cooperation among states.

Notification of planned measures on a shared watercourse is an essential component of the obligation to cooperate and consequently a prerequisite for fulfilment of other substantive obligations. The importance of notification in this regard was reiterated by the ICJ in the 2010 *Pulp Mills Case* in its discussion of the notification requirement of the 1975 Statute of the River Uruguay.[237] 'In the view of the Court, the obligation to inform [the Administrative Commission of the River Uruguay] allows for the initiation of cooperation between the Parties which is necessary in order to fulfil the obligation of prevention'.[238] Cooperation is also thus set forth as the prerequisite for the substantive obligation of prevention.

The obligation to notify is established in Part III, Article 12 of the Convention and specifically requires 'timely notification':

> Before a watercourse State implements or permits the implementation of planned measures which may have a significant effect upon other watercourse States. Such notification shall be accompanied by

234 *Id.*, at 464.
235 *Id.*, at 466.
236 *Id.*, at 470.
237 Statute of the River Uruguay, adopted 26 February 1975, in force 18 September 1976, 1295 UNTS 331, Article 7.
238 *Pulp Mills on the River Uruguay* (*Argentina v. Uruguay*), Judgment, ICJ Reports 2010, p. 14, para. 102.

> available technical data and information, including the results of any environmental impact assessment, in order to enable the notified States to evaluate the possible effects of the planned measures.

The obligation to provide not only notice but also the information upon which to base an assessment of that notices is a codification of the long held and widely understood necessity for this aspect of cooperation. That the assessment of whether an action on the river would have a material effect on a co-riparian is not for the developer to make alone was established as part of the Indus Waters Treaty.

> If either Party plans to construct any engineering work which would cause interference with the waters of any of the Rivers and which, in its opinion, would affect the other Party materially, it shall notify the other Party of its plans and shall supply such data relating to the work as may be available and as would enable the other Party to inform itself of the nature, magnitude and effect of the work. If a work would cause interference with the waters of any of the Rivers but would not, in the opinion of the Party planning it, affect the other Party materially, nevertheless the Party planning the work shall, on request, supply the other Party with such data regarding the nature, magnitude and effect, if any, of the work as may be available.[239]

It is also important to note that the obligation to notify is not limited to the upstream state's activities that could potentially cause a more corporeal harm to the quality or quantity of the water itself. Activities by a downstream state that may result in a later claim of acquired rights thereby foreclosing an upstream state's legal right to develop the watercourse likewise fall within the notification requirement.[240]

Iraq's assertion that Turkey failed to comply with the requirement to consult and give prior notice, much less cooperation, in the Ilisu Dam project has been a source of controversy. One policy paper authored by the Save the Tigris and

239 The Indus Waters Treaty 1960 between the Government of India, the Government of Pakistan and the International Bank for Reconstruction and Development, adopted 19 September 1960, in force 12 January 1961, 419 UNTS 125, Article VII (2).

240 S. M. A. Salman, '*Notification Concerning Planned Measures on Shared Watercourses*,' 4(2) Brill Research Perspectives in International Water Law (2020), at 5.

Save the Iraqi Marshes campaign cites Turkey's failure to consult with communities within Iraq directly affected by the Ilisu Dam.[241]

When a state simply declines to either be bound by these fundamental norms and obligations of international law or insists upon viewing the circumstances through its own unique lens, it becomes difficult to protect the rights of other riparian states.

6.4.5 Fundamental Norms and Obligations at the Court of Public Opinion

World Bank funding for major projects is contingent on adherence to the fundamental norms discussed above. One could say that the World Bank policy for funding such projects is the most far reaching and effective set of rules. 'Indeed it stands out as the only international instrument dealing with shared waterways that is a fairly comprehensive one, and with a global reach and practical application.'[242] With respect to the Ilisu Dam, most international sources of funding were withdrawn in the face of the potential catastrophic effects of the dam on both downstream riparian states and the city of Hasankeyf.[243] Turkey was nonetheless able to find enough resources to follow through with completion of the project.

6.5 *Other Ideas?*

6.5.1 The UN Security Council

Turkey's impoundment of water behind the Ilisu Dam has been called by some a weaponization of water in that it will be able to impact the survival of the Iraqi people through its control of the Tigris River. Now during a time when ready access to water for sanitation is more important than ever, Turkey's capacity to manipulate water supplies has been on display. As the COVID-19 pandemic took hold in Kurdish-held northern Syria, Turkey has been

241 Save the Tigris and Iraqi Marshes Campaign, '*Ilisu Dam and Legal Considerations in Iraq*', Policy paper presented to the Iraqi government (22 March 2014), https://www.iraqicivilsociety.org//wp-content/uploads/2014/04/ILISU-DAM-AND-LEGAL-CONSIDERATIONS-IN-IRAQ-Eng.pdf.

242 S. M. A. Salman, *The World Bank Policy for Projects on International Waterways: An Historical and Legal Analysis* (Washington, D.C.: The World Bank, 2009), at 236.

243 Amnesty International, '*Governments Withdraw Financial Support for Ilisu Dam in Turkey*', News (7 July 2009), https://www.amnesty.org/en/latest/news/2009/07/governments-withdraw-financial-support-ilisu-dam-turkey-20090707/; International Rivers, '*Victory: European Governments Backing out of Ilisu Dam Project in Turkey*' (22 June 2009), https://archive.internationalrivers.org/de/node/3535, accessed 10 December 2020.

accused of interrupting the water supply from a water station taken during its October 2019 offensive.[244]

The United Nations Security Council is the body responsible for maintaining international peace and security. In order to carry out this mission, it has the unique ability to enforce compliance with its decisions through the use of sanctions or authorization of the use of force. Chapter Seven of the UN Charter contains the articles empowering the Security Council in fulfilling its mission.[245] The Security Council's historical role has been to address interstate armed conflict.

Although this role has expanded somewhat in the last few decades, the Council has yet to take direct action on ecological conditions as an independent threat to international peace and security. In these last decades, however, the Council has begun to acknowledge ecological conditions as a threat to international peace and security. On 31 January 1992 the President of the Council released a statement that included the following language:

> The absence of war and military conflicts amongst States does not itself ensure international peace and security. The non-military sources of instability in the economic, social, humanitarian, and ecological fields have become threats to peace and security. The United Nations Membership as a whole, working through the appropriate bodies, needs to give the highest priority to the solution of these matters.[246]

The issue of how the Council should work through the appropriate bodies seems to be a sticking point in its willingness to directly engage with issues of climate change.

The only other time the United Nations Security Council has become involved in a situation relating to environmental harm was against Iraq. The 1991 UN Security Council Resolution 687 'reaffirmed Iraq's liability under environmental law for any direct loss or damage, including environmental damage

244 Human Rights Watch, '*Turkey/Syria: Weaponizing Water in a Global Pandemic?*' (31 March 2020), https://www.hrw.org/news/2020/03/31/turkey/syria-weaponizing-water-global-pandemic#; M. von Hein, '*Weaponizing Water in Northern Syria?*', Deutsche Welle (25 March 2020), https://p.dw.com/p/3a2QU.

245 United Nations Charter, adopted 26 June 1945.

246 United Nations Security Council, Note by the President of the Security Council, UN Doc. S/23500 (31 January 1992).

and the depletion of natural resources, resulting from Iraq's unlawful invasion and occupation of Kuwait'.[247]

No matter how compelling the apparent threat to international peace and security may be, the political dynamic of the Security Council makes it a less than effective mechanism for problem solving. Five of the Council's fifteen members are permanent members. In order to take action, there must be an affirmative vote from at least nine of the fifteen members. If any one of the permanent members vetoes the action, it will be prevented from going forward. The permanent members of the Council are China, France, Russia, the United Kingdom and the United States. Given that the interest of at least one of these nations is almost always benefitted by the problematic situation, it is difficult to achieve the necessary consensus for action.

Water scarcity is at the root of a cycle of violence and unrest in the region,[248] and Turkey, as a major host country for Syrian refugees, is directly feeling the impact of this cycle.[249] Rather than having to move the people away from the violence caused by water scarcity, it is undeniably more humane and efficient to remediate the scarcity and hopefully preempt the violence.

6.5.2 Saving Face with the 'Victim Pays' Principle

Aversive measures may not be the best approach to managing long-standing conflicts between neighbours who are heavily invested in asserting their sovereignty. Where diplomacy fails, it might be possible to try payments in exchange for compromise.

The *Rhine Salt Case*[250] provides an intriguing set of possibilities for conflict resolution, especially in the face of entrenched notions of territorial sovereignty. This case involved concerns over water quality. The Rhine River provides numerous services to several European countries, including drinking water and water for the irrigation of valuable crops. In this case the levels of salt in the river had reached levels high enough to cause damage to the famous tulip fields of the Netherlands. It was discovered that the manner in which mine

247 United Nations Security Council, Resolution 687 adopted 3 April 1991, UN Doc. S/RES/687 (1991) (8 April 1991).

248 Hammer, *supra* note 174.

249 See UN High Commissioner for Refugees (UNHCR), *Evaluation of UNHCR's Emergency Response to the Influx of Syrian Refugees into Turkey January 2014–June 2015* (Geneva: UN High Commissioner for Refugees, 2015).

250 *Case Concerning the Auditing of Accounts Between the Kingdom of the Netherlands and the French Republic Pursuant to the Additional Protocol of 25 September 1991 to the Convention on the Protection of the Rhine Against Pollution by Chlorides of 3 December 1976*, Arbitral Award of 12 March 2004 (Permanent Court of Arbitration) [Rhine Salt Case].

waste from the French potash mines in Alsace (Mines de Potasse d'Alsace) was disposed of contributed 54% of the total salt levels in the Rhine.[251] The solution to this discharge problem would be that the French mine would have to use a more expensive method of waste disposal. Following several years of disagreement, the riparian states came to the agreement that they would all bear a share of the cost of proper waste disposal. In the end it was the Netherlands that paid the largest percentage of the increased cost of disposal in order to protect its tulip industry.[252]

This 'victim pays principle' may seem counterintuitive at first glance. Why should the one receiving the harm pay to prevent it? When it comes to regulating the use of shared resources, however, it may be the most efficient way to resolve disputes that are often as much about assertions of sovereignty as they are about the actual benefit being realized from the controversial activity. In the situation where the upstream state is less developed and therefore more in need of assistance, the principle is easiest to apply. It is also relevant, however, to the opposite scenario. After all, the no-harm rule and the doctrine of equitable and reasonable use do not prohibit all harm. If the circumstances underlying a particular source of harm are such that it is difficult to parse out the questions of reasonableness or even the causation of the harm, spreading the cost over all of the parties who have an interest in preventing the harm might actually be the best strategy. Allocating the cost of *not* doing business among all interested parties explicitly recognizes the right of the state in question to do business, thereby reducing perceived threats to its sovereignty.

In the case of the Ilisu Dam, it could be said that the international community is an interested party. Climate change, and specifically drought, is the factor underlying instability in the region.[253] This type of regional instability created ripples that are experienced globally whether through the displacement of people from their homes and the resulting waves of refugees, or through increased violence in the form of terrorist activity.[254] The world will also be greatly impoverished by the loss of the Mesopotamian Marshes and by the loss of the city of Hasankeyf. The marshes have found their place on the UNESCO World Heritage List evidencing their intrinsic global value. Hasankeyf also meets multiple criteria for inclusion as a World Heritage Site, and efforts

251 C. De H. V. Villeneuve, '*Western Europe's Artery: The Rhine*', 36 Natural Resources Journal (1996) 441–454, at 446.

252 Rhine Salt Case, *Supra* note 250; see also Brown Weiss et al., *supra* note 229, at 238.

253 Hammer, *supra* note 173; M. A. Youness, '*How Climate Change Contributed to the Conflicts in the Middle East and North Africa*', World Bank Arab Voices blog (10 December 2015), https://blogs.worldbank.org/arabvoices/climate-change-conflict-mena.

254 Hammer, *supra note 173*.

to have it included failed because it is ultimately the national government that can propose the site to UNESCO.[255]

Turkey has invested an enormous amount of capital in the construction of the Ilisu Dam and while it is too late to hope for a halt to the destruction of the area behind the dam, the possibility of limiting its use could be a more realistic aim. While some Turkish sources make the claim that it will be a 'run of the river dam' meant solely for hydropower,[256] others refer to some plans for irrigation. Limiting the dam to the production of hydropower would result in a significant reduction of harm to Iraq while still allowing Turkey to use the dam for its stated primary purpose. It is unfortunately too late for Hasankeyf.

It is safe to say that Iraq is not in a position to share much of any cost that might result from Turkey agreeing not to use the dam as intended. The international community has an interest, however, in the preservation of the marshes and the city of Hasankeyf. The international community likewise has an interest in fostering rather than undermining stability in the region. The water of the TE Basin is not only an integral part of our common history of human civilization, it is also part of the hydrologic cycle upon which all life on Earth depends. Each of us by virtue of being alive is responsible for some impact on the hydrologic cycle.

It is no longer useful or appropriate to leave climate change out of any attempt at regional problem solving. The warming of the planet necessarily means that the availability of fresh water will be further limited in regions that depend on rivers for their water. Climate change is a crisis multiplier and, given the additional threat this poses to downstream states everywhere, the States bearing the most culpability in the cause of climate change should also bear their share of the cost of responding to its effects. The 'victim pays principle' can and should be expanded to include compensation for limits on development. The voices in Turkey who speak in favour of the dam make the argument that it is not fair for more developed states in Europe to deny other states the right to develop their resources.[257] This discussion of fairness is pivotal to the argument in favour of asking those states who would benefit from another state's ceasing of an activity to pay the price for the benefits lost to that state.

Although not the most common approach to using economic policy to address transboundary environmental issues, the 'victim pays' principle is

---

255 D. Bouscaren, '*The UNESCO Site that Never Was*', Sapiens (29 April 2020), https://www.sapiens.org/archaeology/hasankeyf/.

256 Turkish Ministry of Foreign Affairs, 'Ilisu Dam', http://www.mfa.gov.tr/ilisu-dam.en.mfa (no longer a live link as of 30 October 2020).

257 Hockenos, *supra* note 118.

worthy of employment. It has been proposed as a way to address Indonesia's transboundary pollution problem caused by the development and clearing of its peatlands by burning.[258] In Canada and the United States, programmes that pay ranchers for depredation caused by carnivorous wildlife follow a similar economic logic. In this analysis the ill that is being remedied is the lethal removal of predators by ranchers who hope to protect their livestock. It fits into the 'victim pays' model if one perceives the greater community as the victim in that it is losing the benefit from the presence of a diversity of wildlife. Because the society as a whole is in a better position to pay for this preservation, and because ranching is recognized as a way of life for many, it is then fair to pay ranchers not to eliminate predators from their rangeland.[259]

In many situations where the 'greater good' would benefit from the restraint of some otherwise legal activity, this approach is often the most efficient way to achieve the benefit. This is especially so when ideological or political stances have become entrenched and rigid because it allows for the perception that all sides are being made whole and that all sides stand on an equal footing at the bargaining table.

6.5.3 The Human Right to Water

The human right to water (HRW) in international law has undergone an almost inverted evolution. It is as if the foundation for the structure of fundamental human rights is being designed after the staircase was built.

On 3 January 1976 the International Covenant on Economic, Social and Cultural Rights (ICESC) entered into force.[260] Article 11 of the Covenant specifies that the state parties recognize 'the right of everyone to an adequate standard of living including adequate food, clothing, and housing'. Article 12 recognizes the right of all people to 'attain the highest level of physical and mental health', including that which is necessary for the 'improvement of all aspects of environmental and industrial hygiene'. Although food and hygiene are mentioned specifically in these articles, water is not. In developing the Covenant, it may be that the need for water, like air, seemed too obvious a

---

258 E. Emba, '*Indonesia's Haze: Should the Victims Pay the Polluters?*', The Diplomat (15 July 2016), https://thediplomat.com/2016/07/indonesias-haze-should-the-victims-pay-the-polluters/.

259 University of Alberta, '*Reimbursing Ranchers for Livestock Killed by Predators Supports Conservation Efforts: Compensation Program Offsets Costs of Preserving Wildlife Habitat on Private Land*', Science Daily (17 January 2018), https://www.sciencedaily.com/releases/2018/01/180117152459.htm.

260 United Nations, International Covenant on Economic, Social and Cultural Rights, adopted 16 December 1966, in force 3 January 1976, 993 UNTS 3.

prerequisite for an adequate standard of living and to improved hygiene to be worthy of mention.

Regardless of why water was left out of the Covenant, and in light of 'the widespread denial of the right to water in developing as well as developed countries', the UN Committee on Economic and Social Rights adopted General Comment 15 in November 2002.[261] General Comment 15 makes it clear that the right to water is inherent in Articles 11 and 12 of the Covenant, more specifically, 'sufficient, safe, acceptable, physically accessible and affordable water for personal and domestic uses'. The United States, although a signatory, never ratified the ICECSC.

Later, in 2010, the UN General Assembly and the UN Human Rights Commission adopted a resolution recognizing the human right to water.[262] In spite of this right being a prerequisite to all other rights, including life, several of the more economically developed nations did not sign on.[263] This was likely out of fear of massive financial obligations.

It is not entirely clear how this right is to be implemented. Rights guaranteed under the Covenant on Civil and Political Rights (ICCPR) are subject to immediate application whereas rights under ICESC may be implemented progressively as states make good faith efforts to develop their capacity.[264] General Comment 15 refers to ICESC, however, given that to deprive a population of water would be to sentence it to death, it seems that the human right to water might be more appropriately subsumed within the ICCPR.[265] Whether the human right to water is a right that must be implemented immediately or whether it is a right that can be implemented progressively, the fact that human beings have a right to water is incontrovertible.

It is difficult to formulate a rational argument that there could be a right to life without a right to the water necessary to sustain that life. It would seem that the question of whether or not there is a right to water is less controversial than how it is to be enforced and by whom. Even more uncertain is the role of the human right to water in interstate conflicts. While a state would be obliged

261 United Nations Economic and Social Council, General Comment No. 15 (2002): The right to water (arts 11 and 12 of the International Covenant on Economic, Social and Cultural Rights), UN Doc. E/C.12/2002/11 (20 January 2003), para. 1.

262 UNGA, Resolution 64/292 The human right to water, adopted 28 July 2010, UN Doc. A/RES/64/292 (3 August 2010).

263 S. C. McCaffrey, '*The Human Right to Water: A False Promise?*', 47 University of the Pacific Law Review (2016) 221–232, at 227.

264 *Id.*, at 228.

265 *Id.*

to provide water for its people, are there obligations on states with respect to people in other states? If so, what are the delimitations of these obligations?

7 Collaboration, Cooperation and Water Diplomacy

The last few years have seen a global rise in nationalism and isolationism.[266] Leaders in many parts of the world are rejecting the kind of international collaboration necessary to undertake the complex multilateral actions needed to successfully address issues relating to any shared resource.[267] For the most part they are populist leaders elected for their promises to relieve the burdens of the everyman. They elevate policies supporting sovereignty over those supporting sustainability. They generate support for these policies by fostering xenophobia and competition rather than openness and collaboration. These policies threaten to undermine any progress toward global problem solving. In many cases, their populist rhetoric is belied by the fact that they also dismantle local rules that serve to keep the populations within the nation's borders safe. Among many such examples in the United States, the Trump administration is dismantling at least 100 environmental regulations, including several designed to keep consumers and workers safe from toxins.[268] A nationalist approach to international relations is the antithesis of the cooperative and collaborative approach necessary for managing problems that do not recognize borders or national identities.

Significantly, the rise in nationalism coincides with the explosion of the Syrian refugee crisis, and its roots in one of the more dire effects of anthropogenic climate change.[269] Researchers attribute the war in Syria to one of the worst droughts in the country's history.[270] For three years, from 2007–2010, Syria experienced the worst drought on the instrumental record.[271] The ongoing

266 J. Snyder, '*The Broken Bargain: How Nationalism Came Back*', Foreign Affairs (March/April 2019).

267 R. Hersher, '*U.S. Formally Begins to Leave the Paris Climate Agreement*', National Public Radio (4 November 2019), https://www.npr.org/2019/11/04/773474657/u-s-formally-begins-to-leave-the-paris-climate-agreement; BBC News, '*Amazon Rainforest Belongs to Brazil, Says Jair Bolsonaro*', BBC News (24 September 2019), https://www.bbc.com/news/world-latin-america-49815731.

268 N. Popovich, et al., '*The Trump Administration is Reversing 100 Environmental Rules. Here's the Full List*', The New York Times (15 July 2020).

269 C. E. Kelley et al., 'Climate Change in the Fertile Crescent and Implications of the Recent Syrian Drought', 112(11) *PNAS* (17 March 2015) 3241–3246.

270 *Id.*

271 *Id.*

drought, combined with water use policies that exacerbated the water shortage, resulted in crop failures that drove farmers from their fields and into the cities.[272] Approximately 1.5 million people migrated from rural farmland into the urban areas adding demand to resources already strained by high population growth and an influx of refugees from Iraq between 2003 and 2007.[273] The lack of resources created tensions which eventually led to the uprising against Syrian president Bashar al-Assad in 2011. The resulting civil war caused thousands to flee and move into other countries, creating both real and perceived pressure on the local resources, which sparked new tensions and created fertile ground for the seeds of xenophobia, nationalism and isolationism. Seizing the opportunity, politicians have leveraged these social problems to their advantage, cementing their hold on power with promises to protect the sovereignty of their states. It is precisely this kind of approach to international relations that undermines the potential to establish collaborative efforts to solve some of the gravest problems of our time.

Hopefully this rise in nationalism, for the most part, represents only a large and vocal minority rather than a majority of public opinion. However, the repercussions of a failure to collaborate globally threaten to create a global feedback loop of crisis in terms of population movement, protectionism and failure to avert the next crisis. Like the carbon dioxide released from the thawing permafrost, these conditions left unchecked will exacerbate themselves and threaten the liveability of Earth.

The framework of collaborative problem solving as opposed to the mediation of adversarial interests has a long history of use in a variety of fields. It is the embrace of a common objective regardless of disparate views of the best way to achieve that objective. This approach, for example, has long been recognized as the most effective approach to address challenges faced by stakeholders in public education. In the development and implementation of programming for students with disabilities, the employment of collaborative practice and the involvement of all stakeholders are required by law in the United States.[274] More recently, collaborative practice and problem solving have become buzzword for managing conflict in a number of areas, from interoffice disputes to improving the relationship between regulatory agencies and public stakeholders.

The distinction between the theories of limited territorial sovereignty and community of interests can be analogized to the difference between

---

272 Fountain, *supra* note 84.

273 Kelley et al., *supra* note 269.

274 *Individuals with Disabilities Education Act*, 101st United States Congress (18 June 1990).

cooperation and collaboration. Collaboration refers to the collective establishment of and effort toward the achievement of a common goal, whereas cooperation refers to the exchange of support to achieve separate goals. Collaboration is the antithesis of competition in that all participants are working toward a singular purpose and can only benefit from the successes of their neighbours.

Solidarity among stakeholders is the underpinning of this singular purpose. Returning to the *Rhine Salt Mines Case*, the Tribunal there set forth that "[w]hen the States bordering an international waterway decide to create a joint regime for the use of its waters, they are acknowledging a 'community of interests' which leads to a 'community of law.'"[275]

Global ecological conditions, now more than ever, call for concerted action to maintain or even replace the natural resources over which states have previously fought. The ultimate effects of climate change will have a global impact. Whether it is the direct experience of displacement caused by sea level rise or drought, or if the impact is felt through an influx of refugees into new communities, no place will be left unaffected. Combatting and reversing the effects of climate change is perhaps the most representative example of a goal toward which the international community must take a collaborative approach. The unifying interest is the continued habitability of Earth. Maintaining the health of a shared watercourse upon which the ecosystems that support millions of lives depends, is a unifying interest of the same gravity even if on a more regional scale.

7.1 *The Senegal River Example*

Examples of the kind of international collaboration needed to successfully share an international resource provide a valuable roadmap for the development of regimes in areas such as the TE Basin. Multistate basin-wide agreements should be the best mechanisms for the development of a transboundary watercourse.[276] Whether such agreements are binding and capable of being fully realized depends on the ability of the states involved to successfully collaborate. There are unfortunately few examples of such collaboration.[277] 'An overdeveloped sense of national sovereignty seemed to prevent the establishment of effective international river basin organizations'.[278]

275 Rhine Salt Case, *supra* note 250, para. 97.

276 T. Parnall & A. E. Utton, '*The Senegal Valley Authority: A Unique Experiment in International River Basin Planning*', 51(2) Indiana Law Journal (1976) 235–256, at 236.

277 *Id.*, at 236.

278 *Id.*

In the developing world, multistate collaborations in the management of resources valuable to the developed world, such as the Organization of Petroleum Exporting Countries, have proven to be a 'dramatic lesson in the effectiveness of international cooperation'.[279] The management of the Senegal River Basin stands out as a model of such collaboration and demonstrates the benefits of elevating the common good over concerns of sovereignty.

The example of the Senegal River regime is an outlier in its successful establishment and implementation of a collaborative water sharing regime. It represents a model approach in the sharing of a transnational watercourse.

> More than any other African river, the Senegal has been characterized and governed by the most progressive and articulated legal regime. The leitmotif since the inception of this legal regime has been to engage in an experiment that not only follows the most advanced concepts of integrated water resources management, but may also offer lessons in cooperation at the global level.[280]

Its success is evidenced by its very persistence as the mechanism for water resource management in the region, even during times of conflict.[281] It is one that could hopefully be followed in other regions where strife is being caused by a failure to coordinate activities on a shared basin.

The Senegal River Basin (SRB) in West Africa covers 1.6% of the continent.[282] Second only to the Niger in terms of its importance as a West African watercourse, the Senegal River is a transboundary watercourse with a range that extends through four states: Guinea, Mali, Mauritania and Senegal.[283]

In the decades after their independence in 1960, these states began to develop a number of agreements governing the water of the SRB. States of the Senegal River Basin developed a water charter to address equitable allocation, damage to fish stocks and damage to flood recession agricultural practices.[284]

---

279 *Id.*, at 235.

280 M. M. Mbengue, '*A Model for African Shared Water Resources: The Senegal River Legal System*', 23(1) Review of European Community & International Environmental Law (2014) 59–66, at 59.

281 *Id.*

282 K. Frenken, *Irrigation Potential in Africa: A Basin Approach* (Rome: FAO, 1997), Senegal River Basin, http://www.fao.org/3/W4347E/w4347e0h.htm.

283 Mbengue, *supra* note 280.

284 McCaffrey (2007), *supra* note 25, at 272–275.

In 1963, Guinea, Mali, Mauritania and Senegal signed the Convention Relating to the General Development of the Senegal River Basin.[285] This agreement recognized the river's international status, and established the Interstate Committee to manage the river.[286] Prior to adoption of the Convention, the river's international status was not recognized as it had previously been under the control of a single colonial power.[287] Such recognition provided the landlocked country of Mali with the right to navigate the Senegal.[288] The Convention was the first step in creating a system of management based on collaboration and mutual benefit rather than the prioritization of national sovereignties and rights to unilateral actions. In this regard, the system of management is politically advanced even by today's standards.

Nearly a decade later, Mali, Mauritania and Senegal entered into two similarly advanced agreements on the management of the basin's water. On 11 March 1972, the riparian states, minus Guinea, entered into the Convention on the Status of the Senegal River in which the requirement for unanimous approval was established.[289] This requirement is laid out in Article 4:

> No project which is likely to bring about serious modification on the characteristics of the river's regime, on its navigation conditions, the agricultural and industrial exploitation of the river, the sanitary state of the waters, the biological characteristics of its fauna and flora, as well as its water level, will be implemented without the prior approval of the contracting states.[290]

The three states also signed the Convention Establishing the Organization for the Development of the Senegal River. Article 4 of that Convention makes projects on the Senegal subject to the unanimous approval of member states.[291] This represents a much higher requirement of cooperation than that of the

---

285 Convention relating to the General Development of the Senegal River Basin, adopted 26 July 1963, Bamako, Mali.

286 U. Alam & O. Dione, *West Africa—A Regional Approach to Reducing Poverty in the Senegal River Basin* (The World Bank, 2004), http://documents1.worldbank.org/curated/en/458151468767391401/pdf/307660WestoAfriver01see0als00307591.pdf; Mbengue, *supra* note 280.

287 Mbengue, *supra* note 280.

288 *Id.*

289 Convention relating to the Status of the Senegal River, adopted 11 March 1972, Nouakchott, Mauritania.

290 Ibid.

291 Convention Establishing the Organization for the Development of the Senegal River, adopted 11 March 1972, Nouakchott, Mauritania.

1997 UN Watercourses Convention's provision to notify exchange information and consult.

Such systems of management are still unusual. In the case of the SRB, a lack of resources may have precipitated the collaboration among, rather than competition between, states.[292] It was, in part, the search for funds that necessitated a joint approach to management. This may have been a factor that differentiated the situation from the more typical scenario that involves competition between states for scarce resources. More often than not the focus remains on sovereignty and increasing the resource allocation for individual states, rather than the total benefit for all states.[293] Barriers to this kind of collaboration are often based in a lack of trust between states sometimes rooted in millennia of conflict.[294]

The benefits of building on this type of collaborative framework for managing an international river are evident in the example set by Mali, Mauritania and Senegal in the 1972 establishment of the Organisasion pour la Mise en Valeur du fleuve Senegal (OMVS), also known as l'espace OMVS.[295] Considered to be a 'milestone in history', this agreement created a committee for the development and joint ownership of dams on the river.[296] Joint operation of the Manantali Dam by the OMVS countries has increased both hydroelectric power supply and irrigation potential for each of them.[297] This increase in power and agricultural production spurs economic development and benefits in the entire region.[298] The focus of the collaboration is in the sharing of benefits provided by the project, rather than an equitable distribution of the water itself.[299] This approach, known as 'the principle of benefit sharing', is now being promoted by the international donor community.[300]

Development on an international river is never free of ecological liabilities. In the case of dams built on the Senegal River, for example, the Manantali Dam was built to generate much needed electricity in Mali, and other dams reduced the flow of the river to such a degree that ocean saltwater would intrude upstream during the dry months. The Diala Dam, which was built to prevent

292 Mbengue, *supra* note 280, at 61.

293 Alam & Dione, *supra* note 286.

294 *Id.*

295 *Id.*

296 UN Water, 'The Senegal River', https://www.un.org/waterforlifedecade/water_cooperation_2013/senegal_river.shtml.

297 Alam & Dione, *supra* note 286, at 1.

298 *Id.*

299 *Id.*

300 *Id.*, at 7.

this intrusion, has been so effective as to alter the ecosystem of the delta causing an increase in mosquito borne illnesses in the area. These issues are managed in a collaborative manner, however, and the needs of the people of St. Louis, at the mouth of the Senegal, are addressed as are those who depend on the dams further upstream.

Whether the circumstances that facilitated this 'milestone in history' are necessary to the reproduction of this kind of international collaboration is unclear. The economic power of the nations involved is similar[301] and without a stark power imbalance. As noted above, the fact that all of the countries had an overall lack of resources may have been a factor that helped to facilitate this new level of collaboration among nations. Even so, the collaborative development of the Senegal Basin can provide a lesson in possibilities even if the exact circumstances underlying the relationship of the TE Basin states are different. The Senegal Basin states placed the greater good of the region ahead of concerns over sovereignty.[302] Through that, all the states have realized benefits such as the development of a functional physical and institutional infrastructure for water management.[303] In the TE Basin the failure of the states to cooperate has meant that Turkey in many respects is the primary if not sole beneficiary of projects in this basin.

7.2 *Collaboration and the Balance of Power*

Recent developments in the relationship between Iraq and Turkey provide hope that some level of collaboration might be a possibility with regard to water resources in the region. Turkey has an informal agreement with Iraq not to cut off the water supply from the Tigris as it fills the dam, and not to interfere with the Zab River, one of the major tributaries to the Tigris flowing from Turkey.[304] There are also reports of joint projects and 'ongoing cooperation' with Turkey on the filling of the Ilisu. The fact remains, however, that Iraq will remain subject to the will of its upstream neighbours who will have complete control over its source of water. Establishing water security for the future 'will require a collaborative effort between Iraq, Turkey, Syria and Iran ... Some 70% of Iraq's water flows from the three upstream countries, though no formal water sharing agreement exists between them'.[305]

---

301 The World Bank Group, 'GDP Per Capita (current US$) Sub-Saharan Africa' (1960–2019), https://data.worldbank.org/indicator/NY.GDP.PCAP.CD?locations=ZG.

302 Alam & Dione, *supra* note 286, at 2.

303 *Id.*

304 Sattar, *supra* note 102.

305 Issa, *supra* note 86.

Even if the Ilisu Dam in and of itself will not be responsible for the decimation of the Mesopotamian Marshes, it could very well be the proverbial 'last straw'. It will also be the sole cause of much other destruction that will leave tens of thousands of people displaced and the rest of the world greatly impoverished. President Erdogan, in one seat of power or another for decades, may be seeing the beginning of political change in Turkey.[306] Perhaps a moderation of Turkey's politics will be reflected in its approach to the law of international watercourses.

Maintaining stability and good relations between neighbours benefits all sides. Turkey acknowledges that it has a vested interest in a restoration of stability in Iraq.[307] A prerequisite for political stability is access to the resources necessary to support a population, and freedom from the threat that they may be at any moment withdrawn. In this sense, the current need for oil resources in Turkey and the ongoing political difficulties between the United States and Iran may provide a temporary bargaining chip for Iraq. Iraq is rich in oil resources,[308] and has plans to expand exploitation of them.[309] In May 2019, Turkey's waiver that allowed it to buy oil from Iran expired requiring it to find sources elsewhere.[310] Iraq is one of Turkey's main sources of crude oil, and there was already ten billion in bilateral trade between the two countries.[311] In 2019, Iraq's Water Resources Minister, Jamal al-Adily, stated: 'Water should be a link to open trade between the two countries. Turkey will stand to benefit from cooperating with Iraq.'[312]

While somewhat increasing the symmetry of the bargaining relationship, this situation resembles one of mutually assured destruction more than one of symbiotic collaboration. Any such water for oil arrangement is also likely to be temporary. Water and oil are not analogous in terms of their status as a prerequisite to life, and Turkey's need for Iraq's oil is not likely to remain fixed. The political situation may change in the region, enabling Turkey to once again buy oil from Iran. In the future, a gradual weaning from oil consumption in general may also weaken Iraq's bargaining position with regard to oil resources.

306 C. Gall, '*Turkey's President Suffers Stinging Defeat in Istanbul Election Redo*', The New York Times (23 June 2019).

307 Turkish Ministry of Foreign Affairs, 'Relations between Turkey and Iraq', http://www.mfa.gov.tr/relations-between-turkey-and-iraq.en.mfa.

308 Organization of Petroleum Exporting Countries (OPEC), 'OPEC Share of World Crude Oil Reserves, 2018', https://www.opec.org/opec_web/en/data_graphs/330.htm.

309 Issa, *supra* note 86.

310 H. Pamuk, '*Turkey Stopped Purchasing Iranian Oil as of May: Turkish Official*', *Reuters* (22 May 2019), https://www.reuters.com/article/us-turkey-oil-iran-idUSKCN1SS2Z9.

311 Issa, *supra* note 86.

312 *Id.*

Reaching beyond the regional concerns for stability, there is a vested global interest in preventing any place from becoming uninhabitable.

7.3 *Three Snapshots of Sovereignty, Hegemony and Other Barriers to Collaboration*

While examples of successful collaboration are unfortunately rare, there are abundant examples across the globe of disputes among neighbouring states in the sharing of transboundary water courses. In some cases, there exists a combination of relatively recent independence and the end of a centralized system for managing the water over the entire region along with a marked imbalance of economic and political power.

Knowledge of the socio-political history and current milieu of a basin is fundamental to understanding the roots of its troubles with sharing the most essential of resources. In order to devise a functional guide for encouraging collaborative systems of water resource management, it is important to compare the challenges and outcomes of other disputes over transboundary watercourses. In taking this comparative approach, the role of a current imbalance of power reveals itself to be potentially both a stabilizing force, as well as the main factor allowing for acts that result in obvious and egregious injustice. Zeitoun and Warner described these two faces of hegemony as 'guiding hegemony' and 'dominative hegemony'.[313]

7.3.1 The United States and Mexico: the Hatching of the Harmon Doctrine

The Harmon Doctrine is 'virtually synonymous' with the theory of 'absolute territorial sovereignty'.[314] It has never been recognized as a legitimate precept of international law. It is remarkable, in part, by virtue of the fact that it was not fully adhered to by the United States even in resolving the dispute that produced it. In spite of its formal position on the Doctrine, the actions of the United States in resolving this and later disputes belied its supposed embrace thereof.[315]

Following on the heels of the Mexican-American war of 1845, a dispute between the two countries over the waters of the Rio Grande resulted in an opinion that, given its historical context, only makes sense as having been

313 M. Zeitoun & J. Warner, '*Hydro-Hegemony—A Framework for Analysis of Trans-Boundary Water Conflicts*', 8 *Water Policy* (2006) 435–460, at 437.

314 McCaffrey (2007), *supra* note 25, at 77.

315 S. C. McCaffrey, '*The Harmon Doctrine One Hundred Years Later: Buried, Not Praised*', 36 Natural Resources Journal (1996) 965–1007, at 1004–1006.

a tool for political posturing. Following the war the countries signed the Treaty of Guadalupe Hidalgo which required Mexico to cede 55% of its territory to the United States in exchange for 15 million dollars and a guarantee that the property rights of Mexicans within US territory would be protected.[316] The California gold rush of 1848 resulted in many Mexican landowners being nonetheless pushed out.[317] It is in this context that a dispute over water rights developed. The United States, not yet the global power it became during the latter half of the twentieth century, was, through the doctrine of manifest destiny, at the tail end of a rapid expansion.[318]

The Rio Grande extends 1,901 miles, from the San Juan Mountains of Colorado in the United States to the Gulf of Mexico. The river forms the border with Mexico for about 1,255 miles before it empties into the Gulf.[319] In the late nineteenth century, the United States began to promote agricultural development in the dry western states. By 1894 diversions from the Rio Grande used for the irrigation of crops in the southwestern United States had reduced the flow of the river to such a degree that communities in northern Mexico were in danger of complete devastation due to a lack of water.[320] A letter from the Mexican minister at Washington, Matias Romero, which accompanied his transmission of a letter received from Mr. José Zayas Guarneros, the consul of Mexico at El Paso, described the dire urgency of the situation in terms of the annihilation of the Mexican frontier communities.[321] Mr. Guarneros further outlined the impacts of the diversions from the Rio Grande on the American side of the border on the communities on the Mexican side and his concerns over plans for future development.[322]

---

316 U.S. Library of Congress, 'Treaty of Guadalupe Hidalgo: Primary Documents in American History', https://guides.loc.gov/treaty-guadalupe-hidalgo.

317 Council on Foreign Relations, 'U.S.–Mexico Relations 1810–2010', https://www.cfr.org/timeline/us-mexico-relations.

318 J. T. Heidler and D. S. Heidler, '*Manifest Destiny*', Encyclopedia Britannica Online (18 November 2020), https://www.britannica.com/event/Manifest-Destiny.

319 International Boundary & Water Commission, United States Section, 'About the Rio Grande', https://www.ibwc.gov/CRP/riogrande.htm#:~:text=The%20river%20runs%20 1%2C255%20miles,(Brownsville%2F%20Matamoros%20area).

320 U.S. Department of State, Office of the Historian, 'Papers Relating to the Foreign Relations of the United States, 1894, With the Annual Message of the President, Transmitted to Congress, December 3, 1894', https://history.state.gov/historicaldocuments/frus1894/d386.

321 *Id.*

322 *Id.*

> Agriculture, which is already impoverished on this entire frontier, is threatened with total destruction within perhaps two years, if the scarcity of the river water continues during that short period; and the destruction of agriculture will inevitably entail the ruin of the infant industries which are now kept in existence with so much difficulty ... There remains no other recourse for the maintenance of tranquility pending the settlement of the main question—the only one which will remedy so many evils—than the equitable division of the waters of the river.
>
> There is a scarcity of that water here, not because the supply in the river has been naturally exhausted, in which case there would, of course, be no ground for complaint, but because of the numberless drains which have been made by the farmers of Colorado and New Mexico, who have settled the pending question by appropriating the water of the Rio Grande to their own exclusive use.
>
> Companies, moreover, are still being organized and plans are being formed, more or less seriously, for the purpose of monopolizing on the American side the small amount of water brought down by the river in those months when it is so abundant that it can not (sic)be exhausted by the drains in New Mexico and Colorado. A meeting of stockholders has just been held at Denver for the purpose of removing the political and material difficulties which have hitherto stood in the way of the accomplishment of their plans for irrigation, and I am informed that it is attempted to create the impression that these plans involve certain concessions in favor of Ciudad Juarez, such as selling it the water which it requires, when Ciudad Juarez has quite as much right as they have to use the water.
>
> The plans, which have heretofore threatened our city with destruction, are not unknown to you, and it is probable that you also have knowledge of those to which I have referred as having been discussed by the meeting at Denver, but, as a supplement to this report, I have the honor to inclose (sic) four clippings from The Times newspaper, published in this city, which have reference to that meeting, and, as I have already remarked, I leave it to you to consider the consequences that must necessarily follow the accomplishment of those plans.[323]

In determining how to address Mexico's claim to its share of the water of the Rio Grande and its request that the United States reduce its diversions and halt further development, the U.S. State Department, for lack of its own

323 *Id.* (references omitted).

in-house counsel, referred to then U.S. Attorney General Judson Harmon. Attorney General Harmon, a man described in an 1895 newspaper article as having 'little place in his makeup' for compromise,[324] produced a nine-page opinion, within which is contained a two-paragraph section that has come to be known as the Harmon Doctrine. Consisting mainly of a then eighty-year old U.S. Supreme Court opinion in a case about sovereign immunity, the paragraphs read as follows:

> The fundamental principle of international law is the absolute sovereignty of every nation, as against all others, within its own territory. Of the nature and scope of sovereignty with respect to judicial jurisdiction, which is one of its elements, Chief Justice Marshall said (Schooner Exchange v McFaddon, 7 Cranch [U.S. Supreme Court Reports] p. [116, at] p. 163 [(1812)]):
>
> The jurisdiction of the nation within its own territory is necessarily exclusive and absolute. It is susceptible of no limitation not imposed by itself. Any restriction upon it, deriving validity from an external source, would imply a diminution of its sovereignty to the extent of the restriction, and an investment of that sovereignty to the same extension that power which could impose such restriction.
>
> All exceptions, therefore, to the full and complete power of a nation within its own territories must be traced up to the consent of the nation itself. They can flow from no other legitimate source.[325]

The Harmon Doctrine, in setting forth the premise that a country is free to do as it wishes with the waters that flow through its borders without regard to the impacts on its neighbours, was never warmly embraced by the United States even at the time, and is widely disavowed now as a functional approach to international relations. The dispute was eventually resolved without regard for the assertions made by Attorney General Harmon with the adoption of the 1906 Convention Concerning the Equitable Distribution of the Waters of the Rio Grande for Irrigation Purposes in which both countries agreed to an equitable and agreeable apportionment of the waters.[326] In this situation, the rattling of the sovereignty sabre appears to have been more an act of

324 The New York Times, '"Attorney General Judson Harmon" reproduced from The Cincinnati Commercial Gazette (11 June 1895)', https://www.nytimes.com/1895/06/11/archives/attorney-general-judson-harmon.html.

325 21 Op. U.S. Att'y Gen., *supra* note 146, at 281–282.

326 McCaffrey (1996), *supra* note 315, at 995.

advocacy than an establishment of foreign policy. Currently across the globe there are other cases where the reverse is true. In the case of the Ilisu Dam, Iraq and Syria's protests have not prevailed in altering Turkey's course of action. Although it proposes that its projects will benefit its downstream neighbours, Turkey asserts the right to do as it wishes with the rivers and thereby holds all of the power, adhering to the Harmon Doctrine in actions if not words.

7.3.2 China and Its Downstream Neighbours on the Mekong: Upstream Hydro-Hegemony

The People's Republic of China is the upstream neighbour to several countries with which it shares 40 major transboundary watercourses.[327] It has signed treaties with most of its immediate neighbours. Exceptions to this are Bhutan and India.[328] One major and ongoing source of controversy has been China's damming of the Mekong River, known within China as the Lancang.

Rising on the Tibetan Plateau in China and flowing through six countries before emptying into the South China Sea, the Mekong River is depended upon by tens of millions of people for their food and livelihoods.[329] In fact, 20% percent of the world's freshwater fish catch is dependent on the 'monsoonal ebb and flow of the Mekong'.[330]

The Tonle Sap in Cambodia is a lake that is inundated with fresh water during the rainy season, expanding the size of the lake by up to five times.[331] A major part of the region's population depends on fish from this seasonal lake to meet their needs throughout the year. The lake's unique system supports a rich biodiversity, including numerous plant species specifically adapted to the rainy and dry seasons. The flooded forests provide a natural barrier that protects the villages from the seasonal inundations.[332]

Once known as one of the great untamed rivers, the Mekong was a life-giving artery for the heart of Southeast Asia. Rich with silt from the high plateaus it was one of the world's most fertile rivers, supporting agriculture and fisheries

---

327 H. Chen, A. Rieu-Clarke & P. Wouters, '*Exploring China's Transboundary Water Treaty Practice Through the Prism of the UN Watercourses Convention*', 38(2) Water International (2013) 217–230.

328 *Id.*

329 H. Beech, '*China Limited the Mekong's Flow. Other Countries Suffered a Drought*', The New York Times (13 April 2020).

330 B. Eyler, 'Science Shows Chinese Dams are Devastating the Mekong' *Foreign Policy* (22 April 2020).

331 UNESCO, 'Tonle Sap Biosphere Reserve, Cambodia' http://www.unesco.org/new/en/natural-sciences/environment/ecological-sciences/biosphere-reserves/asia-and-the-pacific/cambodia/tonle-sap/.

332 *Id.*

throughout much of the region. Snowmelt from glaciers high on the Tibetan Plateau feeds the river, providing about 30% of the water during the dry season.[333] Because of the effects of climate change, the glaciers are melting and their ability to function as water storage for the Mekong River Basin and other rivers is now threatened.

Over the last 20 years, China has begun building dams on the upper river. The dams are primarily for hydropower, the steep river canyons of the Tibetan Plateau making agriculture unfeasible in the upper river region. Hydropower dams, while generally not affecting the quantity of water downstream, do affect the quality, in that the fertile silt depended upon by farmers is trapped and unable to make its way downstream. In recent years China has increased its development of the upper Mekong. In a possible attempt to compensate for lost glacial water storage, China has held back the river's flow in spite of drought conditions downstream, according to recent research.[334] Though China has pledged to use the dams to regulate flow on the lower Mekong to more evenly distribute high and low flows, the most recent drought has proven this to be a hollow promise.[335] During the most recent drought in the lower Mekong, the river's water level reached critically low levels, completely drying up in some sections,[336] while reports indicate that a normal seasonal water supply was being held back upstream. Millions in Vietnam are without access to fresh water.[337] In some cases the flows are released unpredictably, causing even further destruction downstream. This kind of uncoordinated unilateral development threatens the lives and livelihoods of the tens of millions of people that depend on a living Mekong for their survival. Had there been a cooperative, not to mention collaborative approach among the upper and lower Mekong states, the catastrophic effects of the loss of Mekong water could have been avoided.[338]

---

333 FAO, AQUASTAT *Transboundary River Basin Overview—Mekong* (Rome: FAO, 2011).

334 A. Basist & C. Williams, *Monitoring the Quantity of Water Flowing through the Upper Mekong Basin under Natural (Unimpeded) Conditions* (Bangkok: Sustainable Infrastructure Partnership, 2020), https://558353b6-da87-4596-a181-b1f20782dd18.filesusr.com/ugd/81dff2_68504848510349d6a827c6a433122275.pdf?index=true.

335 *Id.*

336 E. Sasipornkarn, '*A Dam-building Race Threatens the Mekong*', Deutsche Welle (16 August 2019), https://www.dw.com/en/about-dw/profile/s-30688; Beech, *supra* note 329.

337 H. Nam, '*Mekong Delta Struggles to Find Freshwater as Drought, Salt Intrusion Continue*' VNExpress International (22 March 2020), https://e.vnexpress.net/news/news/mekong-delta-struggles-to-find-freshwater-as-drought-salt-intrusion-continue-4071219.html.

338 Basist & Williams, *supra* note 334.

In October 2019, the first lower Mekong Dam began to operate its turbines in the landlocked country of Laos.[339] This accelerated development has resulted in two major problems for the populations that depend on the river. First, the activity has further removed the life-giving silt from the river water resulting in a 'dead' river that cannot sustain aquatic life. Fish populations have declined and communities that once were able to meet their food needs through fishing are now forced to import food from other areas. Second, the water levels themselves have dropped because of activity upstream preventing use of the river downstream for agricultural purposes.

In 1995, the lower Mekong countries, Thailand, Cambodia, Laos and Vietnam, signed the Agreement on the Cooperation for the Sustainable Development of the Mekong River Basin.[340] This agreement established the Mekong River Commission for the purpose of collaborating to 'jointly manage the shared water resources and the sustainable development of the Mekong River'.[341] The Commission also acts as 'a regional knowledge hub on water resources management that helps to inform the decision-making process based on scientific evidence.' Beyond establishing a basis for reasonable and equitable utilization of the water, the Agreement emphasizes a collaborative approach in its first two articles. Article 1 outlines the areas of cooperation as

> all fields of sustainable development, utilization, management and conservation of the water and related resources of the Mekong River Basin including, but not limited to irrigation, hydro-power, navigation, flood control, fisheries, timber floating, recreation and tourism, in a manner to optimize the multiple-use and mutual benefits of all riparians and to minimize the harmful effects that might result from natural occurrences and man-made activities.

Article 2 on projects, programs and planning includes an objective of realizing sustainable benefits for all riparian states: 'To promote, support, cooperate and coordinate in the development of the full potential of sustainable benefits to all riparian States and the prevention of wasteful use of Mekong River Basin waters'.

339 Sasipornkarn, *supra* note 336; Beech, *supra* note 329.

340 Agreement on the Cooperation for the Sustainable Development of the Mekong River Basin, adopted 5 April 1995, Chieng Rai, Thailand.

341 UNOPS *'UNOPS and the Mekong River Commission Enhance Cooperation to Protect Vital Water Resources'* https://www.unops.org/news-and-stories/news/unops-and-the-mekong-river-commission-enhance-cooperation-to-protect-vital-water-resources.

China, notably, is not a party to this agreement. While China and Myanmar, the other riparian state not a party to the agreement, both have the right to enter under Article 39, they currently only participate as 'dialogue partners'.[342] China has, however, developed what can be thought of as its own forum for discussions around the management of the Mekong, the Lancang Mekong Cooperation.[343]

As the world's second largest economy,[344] China holds a great deal of power in the region. As the upstream neighbour to several less powerful states, the term 'hydro-hegemony' has been used to describe China's (and India's) approach to managing regional water resources.[345] Whether the hegemonic control over a resource that is a prerequisite to life itself can be adequately tempered with promises to act benevolently is doubtful, especially when there has been a demonstrated failure to do so. The upstream regional hegemon has especially powerful leverage in that, given a situation without binding treaties or international law, it has absolute control over what could be said is the life force of its downstream neighbours. Another scenario exists, however, in which the regional hegemon is the downstream neighbour and uses the force of existing law and treaties to foreclose development that could benefit its less powerful upstream neighbours. Egypt's relationship with its upstream neighbour Ethiopia is an example of this scenario, which will be discussed below in the next section.

Turkey's relationship to its downstream neighbours is similar in that it has control of the 'spigot' of the source of water for an entire region. The Tonle Sap is drying out, as are the Mesopotamian Marshes. In the case of the Mekong, the causes seem to be somewhat clearer cut, however, because the upstream dams seem to be solely to blame.

---

342 Chen et al., *supra* note 327.

343 Langcang-Mekong Cooperation China Secretariat, '*A Brief Introduction of Lancang-Mekong Cooperation*' (13 December 2017), http://www.lmcchina.org/eng/n3/2020/0904/c416294-9755278.html; S. Wu, '*The Trouble with the Lancang Mekong Cooperation Forum*', The Diplomat (19 December 2018), https://thediplomat.com/2018/12/the-trouble-with-the-lancang-mekong-cooperation-forum/.

344 The World Bank, 'The World Bank in China', https://www.worldbank.org/en/country/china/overview.

345 B. Chellaney, '*China's Water Hegemony*', YaleGlobal Online (5 May 2016), https://yaleglobal.yale.edu/content/chinas-water-hegemony.

7.3.3 Egypt, Sudan, Ethiopia and the Nile: Downstream Hydro-Hegemony

As this monograph is being written, a dispute over the waters of the Nile is coming to a head. In East Africa, the cradle of humankind, where some of the earliest evidence of human life has been found,[346] rise the headwaters of the Blue Nile. Following a pattern of river development, the downstream users in the more arid regions were forced to develop the river earlier in order to build their civilizations whereas users in the upstream regions were able to rely on rainfall to grow crops. For thousands of years Egypt has controlled the waters of the Nile.[347] Egypt has 'through a myriad of mechanisms and tactics' maintained the status of hydro-hegemon in the region.[348] From attempted invasion in the nineteenth century and the threat of force, to a series of colonial era treaties, and a later agreement with Sudan, Egypt has, until recently, been able to foreclose any development of the Nile by its upstream riparians. Leveraging the doctrine of complete territorial integrity, Egypt claims that any decrease in the amount of water it receives will cause harm and that any development of the Nile by Ethiopia poses an existential threat. Ethiopia needs to harness the hydroelectric potential of the dam, however, in order to provide power to the 65 million people who currently live without electricity.[349]

The Nile stretches about 67,000 kilometres and is commonly considered to be the world's longest south to north running river.[350] It is formed by two main tributaries, the Blue Nile originating in the Highlands of Ethiopia, and the White Nile originating on the Equatorial Lakes Plateau. From these humid regions with abundant rainfall the two tributaries run north and down into the arid desert to their confluence at Khartoum, Sudan, after which it is joined by one other tributary, which also originates in Ethiopia. The Nile flows northward from this point through the arid regions of Sudan and Egypt before finally emptying into the Mediterranean Sea near Alexandria. Of the Nile tributaries,

346 E. Hadingham, '*Where is the Birthplace of Humankind? South Africa and East Africa Both Have Claims*', National Geographic (11 September 2015), https://www.nationalgeographic.com/news/2015/09/150911-hominin-hominid-berger-homo-naledi-fossils-ancestor-rising-star-human-origins/.

347 D. Walsh & S. Sengupta, '*For Thousands of Years, Egypt Controlled the Nile. A New Dam Threatens That*', The New York Times (9 February 2020).

348 M. E. Tekuya, '*The Egyptian Hydro Hegemony in the Nile Basin: The Quest for Changing the Status Quo*', 26(1) Journal of Water Law (2018) 10–20, at 10.

349 BBC News, '*River Nile Dam: Reservoir Filling Up Ethiopia Confirms*' (15 July 2020), https://www.bbc.com/news/world-africa-53416277.

350 Although widely accepted as the world's longest river overall, some assert that the Amazon River is actually longer than the Nile. See J. Roach, '*Amazon Longer than Nile River, Scientists Say*', National Geographic (2007).

the Blue Nile contributes significantly more water than the White. The fluctuation the Blue Nile's water supply is dramatic, however, in that it depends on the heavy rains originating from the monsoon season in the Indian Ocean for its supply.[351] By the end of the dry season, its flow has decreased markedly. The White Nile's flow is steadier, and during the Blue Nile's dry season it accounts for about four-fifths of the River's flow.[352]

Egypt and Sudan are among the largest countries in the basin, and they contribute the least amount of its water. Egypt contributes the least amount of water with a minimum of 0 to a maximum of 120 millimetres for a mean of 15 mm of water per year. Sudan by virtue of its less arid far southern regions contributes a mean amount of 500 mm. This can be compared with Ethiopia's mean contribution of 1,125 mm. As a direct consequence of their arid climate, both Egypt and Sudan also rely heavily on the river for their water resources, as much as 97% and 77% respectively.[353]

'Without the Nile there is no Egypt.'[354] Like the relationship of the ancient cultures of Mesopotamia to the Tigris and Euphrates, the Nile has been the lifeblood of Egyptian culture and its sustenance for thousands of years. Nearly 95% of Egypt's population, which now totals over 100 million, lives on a narrow strip of fertile land along the river.[355]

Even though most of the Nile's water originates in Ethiopia, it has not until recently been able to develop the river to its own benefit. Ethiopia's challenge to Egypt's hydro-hegemony has now reached a turning point, and the pressure to defend notions of historical privilege, sovereignty and national pride threaten any stability that may have taken hold in the region.

Progress toward the development of a legal regime that is capable of fostering the reasonable and equitable utilization of the waters of the Nile has been fraught. Historically, it has been through the use of treaties and agreements that Egypt, and before its independence, Britain, secured the waters of the Nile primarily for its use.[356] While only one of these instruments directly involves Ethiopia,[357] the set of agreements, as a whole, has allowed Egypt to be the sole

351 M. M. El-Kammash et al., 'Nile River', Encyclopedia Britannica Online (9 November 2020), https://www.britannica.com/place/Nile-River.

352 McCaffrey (2007), *supra* note 26, at 259.

353 Frenken, *supra* note 282.

354 Walsh & Sengupta, *supra* note 347.

355 D. Walsh, '*As Egypt's Population Hits 100 Million, Celebration is Muted*', The New York Times (11 February 2020).

356 Tekuya, *supra* note 348, at 11.

357 Treaty on the Delimitation of the Frontiers between Ethiopia and Sudan, adopted 15 May 1902, Addis Ababa, Ethiopia.

arbiter of the use of the Nile. Claiming that it is not bound by a 1959 treaty between Egypt and Sudan that divides the Nile's waters primarily between Egypt and Sudan, and following unsuccessful attempts to create a basin-wide mechanism for cooperative and sustainable development, Ethiopia pressed forward with its own plan for development of the river.

The attempts to establish a basin-wide mechanism for cooperation are represented primarily by the 1999 Nile Basin Initiative[358] and the Cooperative Framework Agreement (CFA) over which negotiations disintegrated in 2010. These negotiations

> collapsed after more than ten years of facilitation by the World Bank and some other donors. The collapse resulted from insistence by Egypt and Sudan on inclusion of a specific reference in the CFA to what they consider as their 'acquired rights' over the Nile waters, claiming that such rights represent their vital and absolute 'water security'.[359]

This attempt to leverage 'water security' as a mechanism for enforcing the doctrine of complete territorial integrity failed, and the lack of any agreement left Ethiopia with few other options. Essentially resorting to the tactic of uncoordinated unilateral development, Ethiopia began construction on the Grand Ethiopian Renaissance Dam (GERD) in 2011. A US$4.5 billion hydroelectric project and the largest dam in Africa,[360] the project has been viewed as an existential threat by Egypt. Over the last decade Egypt has protested the construction of the dam, even resorting to the consideration of acts of violence. In 2013, at a meeting hosted by then president Mohammed Morsi, several politicians, unaware that cameras were rolling, were overheard making threats, including using Ethiopian rebels as a bargaining chip and the destruction of the dam itself.[361] Support for the project had already begun to materialize, including backing from Sudan.[362]

Finally, in March of 2015, Ethiopia, Egypt, and Sudan agreed on the Declaration of Principles Agreement containing ten principles concerning international law, four of which are specific to the GERD itself. This agreement

358 Nile Basin Initiative, NBI Overview, https://nilebasin.org/documents-publications/73-nile-basin-initiative-an-overview/file, accessed 10 December 2020.

359 Salman (2020), *supra* note 240, at 4.

360 Africa Ranking, 'Largest Dams in Africa', http://www.africaranking.com/largest-dams-in-africa/2/; D. Walsh, '*As Seasonal Rains Fall, Dispute over Nile Dam Rushes toward a Reckoning*', The New York Times (18 July 2020).

361 J. Fleishman, '*Egypt-Ethiopia Water Dispute Escalates After Threatening Remarks*', The Los Angeles Times (6 June 2013).

362 Tekuya, *supra* note 348, at 15.

can be seen as marking a change in Egypt's hegemonic control of the Nile. It marked an end to the threat of military action as well as Egypt's continued demand that construction of the GERD be halted.[363] Could Ethiopia's actions be seen as a kind of civil disobedience on an international scale? Given the historical power imbalance in the region and the intractability of any process, could the flaunting of some fundamental obligations under international law have been necessary to secure the equitable and reasonable use of the water? In its insistence on its sovereign right to utilize the water within its borders and in the face of Egypt's insistence on the doctrine of absolute territorial integrity, did Ethiopia decide that the answer to such an impasse was to act unilaterally?

In the fall of 2019, as the dam neared completion and with water scarcity already a looming problem in Egypt, tension over the completion of the dam began to mount as fear and national pride began to mingle and turn the discussion once again toward armed conflict. Egypt's population is currently increasing at a rate of one million people every six months, a rate predicted by the United Nations to result in a water shortage by 2025.[364] In addition, predicted changes in climate will likely increase the number of dry years in Egypt. Ethiopia, like Turkey, has responded to this concern with the assertion that it is more suitable to store the water behind dams in their less arid climates where there will be less loss of water through evaporation.[365]

Ethiopia's Prime Minister Abiy Ahmed has facilitated rapid change in a country that has long been plagued by poverty and violence. He was a winner of the 2019 Nobel Peace prize for his work in establishing peaceful relations with neighbouring Eritrea. In September of 2018 he was able to reopen the borders between the two countries.[366] In addition to facilitating rapid sociopolitical change in Ethiopia, Mr. Ahmed has also demonstrated a commitment to environmental sustainability. In 2019, as part of his 'Green Legacy Initiative', Ethiopians planted over 350 million trees in a record-breaking single day.[367] In July 2020, Ethiopia revealed its first locally-built fully electric car.[368]

---

363 S. M. A. Salman, *'How and Why Has the Ethiopian Strategy on Renaissance Dam Succeeded?'* The Citizen (29 March 2015).

364 Walsh & Sengupta, *supra* note 347.

365 *Id.*; see also Bremer, *supra* note 7.

366 BBC News, *'Abiy Ahmed, Ethiopia's Prime Minister'* (11 October 2019), https://www.bbc.com/news/world-africa-43567007.

367 United Nations Environment Programme, *'Ethiopia Plants Over 350 Million Trees in a Day, Setting New World Record'* (2 August 2019), https://www.unenvironment.org/news-and-stories/story/ethiopia-plants-over-350-million-trees-day-setting-new-world-record.

368 A. G. Tadesee, *'Ethiopia Showcases First Locally-Assembled Electric Car'*, Andalou Agency (27 July 2020), https://www.aa.com.tr/en/africa/ethiopia-showcases-first-locally-assembled-electric-car/1924109.

It is against this backdrop of forward-thinking actions that the loggerhead with Egypt and Sudan over the completion of GERD is set. In October 2019, less than two weeks after winning the Nobel Peace Prize, Prime Minister Ahmed warned that 'no force could prevent' the completion of the dam and that he would get 'millions readied' for war with Egypt.[369] In late June and early July 2020, satellite images indicated that the water level behind the dam was rising.[370] On 15 July 2020, following unproductive talks with Egypt and Sudan, these images and the fact that the dam was filling were confirmed by Ethiopia's Water Minister, Seleshi Bekele, using fairly ambiguous language. He stated that the water had begun to fill the reservoir 'in line with the natural process' and that '[t]he construction of the dam and the filling of the water go hand in hand'.[371] Three days later, on 18 July, Mr. Bekele tempered his statement, stating that the rise in the water level behind the dam was due to the current seasonal flooding, and the process of closing the dam in order to impound water behind it had not yet begun.[372] On 21 July 2020, talks facilitated by the African Union resumed.[373] On 22 July, Prime Minister Abiy Ahmed announced that the first year target for filling the dam had been reached. The waters had begun to overtop the dam, which is still under construction. Water Minister Seleshi Bekele said that this would allow for the first set of turbines to be tested.[374] On 5 August, Egypt and Sudan suspended talks with Ethiopia over Ethiopia's suggestion that an agreement be linked to a broader agreement on the Blue Nile.[375] On 15 August, Pope Francis, during his Angelus Message for Assumption Day, urged the parties to resume talks 'so that the eternal river will continue to be a source of life, which unites and does not divide, which nurtures friendship, prosperity and fraternity and not enmity, misunderstanding and

369 Walsh & Sengupta, *supra* note 347.

370 BBC News (15 July 2020), *supra* note 349.

371 *Id.*

372 Walsh (18 July 2020), *supra* note 360.

373 African Union, '*Communique of the 2nd Extraordinary African Union (AU) Bureau of the Assembly of Heads of State and Government Videoteleconference Meeting on the Grand Ethiopian Renaissance Dam (GERD)*' (24 July 2020), https://au.int/en/pressreleases/20200724/hosg-communique-2nd-meetinng-grand-ethiopian-renaissance-dam-gerd.

374 BBC News (15 July 2020), *supra* note 349.

375 S. Magdy, '*Egypt, Sudan Suspend Talks with Ethiopia over Disputed Dam*' Associated Press (5 August 2020), https://apnews.com/article/ethiopia-sudan-middle-east-africa-egypt-b8fb2ee6360473cf6c7e28919410ecd6.

conflict'.[376] On 16 August 2020, the three countries returned to the table and agreed to continue talks the following week.[377]

Through the lens of hundreds of years of Egyptian control, a history of mistrust, enormous expenditures and national pride, leaders of Ethiopia, Egypt and Sudan must find a path to a resolution while preserving their credibility as leaders for their people. Is there a mechanism that can allow for a 'face-saving' path to collaboration?

Turkey, in objecting to Iraq and Syria's assertion of acquired rights, alluded to the fact that the doctrine of absolute territorial integrity is disfavoured and defended its unilateral actions in building and filling the Ilisu Dam. Comparing the TE Basin to the Nile Basin, however, one encounters an entirely different set of facts. In the case of the Nile Basin, Egypt, the downstream county, has held the bulk of the political power in the region and has had the opportunity to develop the river while preventing Ethiopia from doing the same. The Ilisu Dam, the last of several of Turkey's developments in the TE Basin, cannot be compared to the GERD, which is Ethiopia's first major development on the Blue Nile. Ethiopia's unilateral action in completing and filling the dam could be said to be due in part to the unequal power dynamic between it and Egypt, whereas that would be a difficult assertion for Turkey to make against Iraq and Syria.

All three of the above examples of disputes over projects on transboundary watercourses are marked by the presence of a power imbalance, as well as an embrace of inequitable approaches to resource allocation. Their differences are in the underlying relationship between the riparians. In regions where lack of water has been a long-standing issue for old neighbours, as with Egypt, the status quo has been enforced by the more powerful state and proposals to make changes have created the friction. In the TE Basin, the region's ongoing conflict over the last decades has made a status quo of any kind difficult to identify. The United States and Mexico were both relatively new states at the end of the nineteenth century, making the water conflicts between them somewhat similar to those newly independent states of the TE Basin. Both were/are in the process of attempting to establish a favourable regime. China's damming of the Mekong represents a new problem in a region where millions of people have lived in and depend upon a water rich environment.

---

376 G. Segreti, '*Pope Francis Calls for Dialogue between Egypt, Ethiopia and Sudan over Nile Dam*', Reuters (15 August 2020), https://www.reuters.com/article/us-ethiopia-dam-pope-idUSKCN25B0KJ.

377 S. Magdy, '*Egypt, Ethiopia, Sudan Resume AU-Led Talks over Disputed Dam*', Associated Press (16 August 2020), https://apnews.com/article/addis-ababa-sudan-middle-east-africa-ethiopia-4f09ddb6a500e2617685d78f102a35d0.

8 Conclusion: Global Solutions for Global Resources

A great deal of writing has been produced acknowledging the need for a trilateral agreement in the development of a comprehensive regime governing the TE Basin. Recent efforts on the part of Syria, Iraq, and Turkey to develop agreements do provide some cause for optimism.[378] The uncoordinated and unilateral approach taken by Turkey in its filling of yet another large dam belies this hopefulness to some extent. In addition to this, the overall institutional framework for successfully managing the basin has yet to be developed. The lack of regularized institutions and systems for data collection and sharing are a barrier to successful negotiation and agreement.[379]

Accompanying the very real fear that increased water scarcity will lead to more conflict, war, and human tragedy, is another view that wars over water are really more about sovereignty and national identity.[380] These views are not mutually exclusive as the feedback loop of war, human displacement, and scarcity feeds the fears of neighbouring countries and provides fodder for the boilers of nationalism and xenophobia. The existence of a stark regional power imbalance cannot be overlooked in the analysis of how and why a dispute over management of a transboundary water resource takes a particular course. The very ability of an upstream riparian to take control of a basin's water resources certainly represents, in itself, a power imbalance. The ability of a downstream riparian to foreclose the access of the upstream neighbour represents the existence of an underlying imbalance of a different nature. Global power dynamics are fluid to some extent, however, and the regional hegemon, having a self-interested motive to maintain stability, is also vulnerable to the upheaval that can be caused by scarcity.

Turkey is not likely to easily release its grasp on the water supply along with the powerful 'upper hand' in the region. Whether a collaborative effort such as the Senegal River Basin regime can take hold in the TE Basin would depend largely on finding incentives for Turkey to remove its hand from the tap. Whether that is through investment in alternatives to hydropower, or the establishment of infrastructure for data collection and sharing, the international community, especially the wealthier nations who have benefitted from both their colonial pasts and from the early exploitation of the resources we all

378 Kirschner & Tiroch, *supra* note 36, at 393.

379 Ünver & Kibaroglu, *supra* note 164, at 11.

380 J. Kalpakian, *Identity, Conflict and Cooperation in International River Systems* (Routledge, 2017).

now seek to preserve, have both an interest and a responsibility to work with Turkey so that it may cede some of its hold on power to its neighbours.

'A riparian's position can be cooperative or conflict-prone. If interdependence is not a sufficient condition for cooperation and may even result in conflict, international regimes may provide the necessary linkage.'[381] Creative solutions to a complex problem involving ancient rivalries, fragile sovereignties, and deep mistrust include application of an expansion of principals similar to those of the 'victim pays principle' discussed above. The international community has an interest in reducing the potential for unrest caused by a lack of water and the resulting mass migration of people, as well as the preservation of the marshes. All parties receiving a benefit from the restrictions placed on one party should bear a portion of the expense. Whether it is an equitable and reasonable use to store water behind a dam for power, while marshlands wither and families become climate refugees, is questionable. Whether the building of dams can indeed provide regional benefits in the face of climate change is also debatable. In an inherently interconnected world and when dealing with the most fluid of resources, it is no longer appropriate to leave the dispute over water resources exclusively with the states through which that water might briefly pass through.

Acknowledgements

I would like to express my deepest gratitude to Dr. Stephen McCaffrey, Distinguished Professor of Law at The University of the Pacific McGeorge School of Law for the knowledge, inspiration and guidance provided to me in the development of this monograph. I would also like to thank my father, Dr. Stephen Thaman, Professor Emeritus of St. Louis University School of Law, who taught me that the practice and scholarship of law is best directed to the benefit of vulnerable and underrepresented people. I would finally like to thank Dr. Norman Stewart, Professor Emeritus of the University of Wisconsin Milwaukee Department of Geography, who introduced me to the study of conservation (even though he strongly advised me that an adversarial legal system is not the best way to help the environment).

381 Ünver & Kibaroglu, *supra* note 164, at 22.

Author Biography

Raquella Moea Thaman is an attorney and teacher in the San Francisco Bay Area. She holds a Juris Doctorate from the University of the Pacific McGeorge School of Law in Sacramento, CA, and a Master of Sciences degree in Education from California State University, Hayward. As an advocate for children's rights she has worked to protect the civil rights of children and young adults with disabilities. At the University of Istanbul's Crime and Punishment Film Festival in 2013, she presented a paper on the over-incarceration of children with disabilities in the United States. Dedicated to preserving our natural resources for future generations, in 2019 she earned an LLM in International Environmental and Water Law from the University of the Pacific McGeorge.

Bibliography

Aboulenein, T. K., '*Turkey halts Filling Tigris Dam after Iraq Complains of Water Shortages*', Reuters (7 June 2018), https://www.reuters.com/article/us-iraq-turkey/turkey-halts-filling-of-ilisu-dam-until-july-ambassador-to-iraq-idUSKCN1J320X.

AFP, '*Drought Puts Iraq at Risk of More Extremism*', Gulf News (2 September 2018).

African Union, '*Communique of the 2nd Extraordinary African Union (AU) Bureau of the Assembly of Heads of State and Government Videoteleconference Meeting on the Grand Ethiopian Renaissance Dam (GERD)*' (24 July 2020), https://au.int/en/press releases/20200724/hosg-communique-2nd-meetinng-grand-ethiopian-renaissance-dam-gerd.

Agreement on the Cooperation for the Sustainable Development of the Mekong River Basin, 5 April 1995, Chiang Rai, Thailand, Mekong River Commission.

Al-Ansari, N. K., S. Knutsson & A. A. Ali, '*Restoring the Garden of Eden, Iraq*', 2(1) Journal of Earth Sciences and Geotechnical Engineering (2012) 53–88.

Al-Zahery, N. E. et al., '*In Search of the Genetic Footprints of Sumerians: A survey of Y chromosome and mtDNA Variation in the Marsh Arabs of Iraq*', 11 BMC Evolutionary Biology (2011) article number 288.

Alam, U., & O. Dione, *West Africa—A Regional Approach to Reducing Poverty in the Senegal River Basin* (The World Bank, 2004).

Ali, L., '*In Basra: Oil in Abundance, but Little Water to Drink*', UNICEF Connect blog (16 July 2019), https://blogs.unicef.org/blog/basra-oil-abundance-little-water-drink/.

Amnesty International, '*Governments Withdraw Financial Support for Ilisu Dam in Turkey*', News (7 July 2009), https://www.amnesty.org/en/latest/news/2009/07/governments-withdraw-financial-support-ilisu-dam-turkey-20090707/.

Arraf, J., '*Months of Protests Roil Iraq's Oil Capital Basra*', National Public Radio (27 September 2018).

Badawi, T., '*Iran's Upstream Hegemony and its Water Policies towards Iraq*', Italian Institute for International Political Studies Commentary (26 February 2020), https://www.ispionline.it/en/pubblicazione/irans-upstream-hegemony-and-its-water-policies-towards-iraq-25173.

Basist, A., & C. Williams, *Monitoring the Quantity of Water Flowing Through the Upper Mekong Basin Under Natural (Unimpeded) Conditions* (Bangkok: Sustainable Infrastructure Partnership, 2020).

BBC (Director). (2019). *Our Water Pollution is a Cancer* [Motion Picture].

BBC News, '*Abiy Ahmed, Ethiopia's Prime Minister*' (11 October 2019), https://www.bbc.com/news/world-africa-43567007.

BBC News, '*U.S. Formally Begins to Leave the Paris Climate Agreement*', National Public Radio (4 November 2019), https://www.bbc.com/news/world-latin-america-49815731.

BBC News, '*River Nile Dam: Reservoir Filling Up Ethiopia Confirms*' (15 July 2020), https://www.bbc.com/news/world-africa-53416277.

Beech, H., '*China Limited the Mekong's Flow. Other Countries Suffered a Drought*', The New York Times (13 April 2020).

Belkis, W., *Basra is Thirsty: Iraq's Failure to Manage the Water Crisis* (Human Rights Watch, 2019).

Bouscaren, D., '*The UNESCO Site that Never Was*', Sapiens (29 April 2020), https://www.sapiens.org/archaeology/hasankeyf/.

Bremer, N., *The Regulation of the Non-Navigational Use of the Euphrates and Tigris River System* (The Hague: Eleven International Publishing, 2017).

Brown, P., '*Dam Backup Plan for Glacier Ice Loss*', Climate News Network (1 June 2016), https://climatenewsnetwork.net/dam-back-up-plan-for-glacier-ice-loss/.

Brown Weiss, E. et al., *International Environmental Law and Policy* (Gaithersburg, MD: Aspen Law & Business, 1998).

Case Concerning the Auditing of Accounts Between the Kingdom of the Netherlands and the French Republic Pursuant to the Additional Protocol of 25 September 1991 to the Convention on the Protection of the Rhine Against Pollution by Chlorides of 3 December 1976, Arbitral Award of 12 March 2004 (Permanent Court of Arbitration).

Case Relating to the Territorial Jurisdiction of the International Commission of the River Oder (United Kingdom v. Poland), Judgment No. 16, 1929 PCIJ (ser. A) No. 23 (September 10).

Chellaney, B., '*China's Water Hegemony*', YaleGlobal Online (5 May 2016), https://yaleglobal.yale.edu/content/chinas-water-hegemony.

Chen, H., A. Rieu-Clarke & P. Wouters, '*Exploring China's Transboundary Water Treaty Practice Through the Prism of the UN Watercourses Convention*', 38(2) Water International (2013) 217–230.

Convention Establishing the Organization for the Development of the Senegal River, adopted 11 March 1972, Nouakchott, Mauritania.

Convention on the Law of the Non-navigational Uses of International Watercourses, adopted 21 May 1997, in force 17 August 2014, 2999 UNTS.

Convention relating to the General Development of the Senegal River Basin, adopted 26 July 1963, Bamako, Mali.

Convention relating to the Status of the Senegal River, adopted 11 March 1972, Nouakchott, Mauritania.

de Onis, J., '*A Step into the 20th Century*', The New York Times (15 July 1973).

De H. V. Villeneuve, C., '*Western Europe's Artery: The Rhine*', 36 Natural Resources Journal (1996) 441–454.

Edzard, D. O. et al., '*History of Mesopotamia*', Encyclopedia Britannica Online (22 October 2019), https://www.britannica.com/place/Mesopotamia-historical-region-Asia.

Edzard, D. O. et al., '*Mesopotamia to the End of the Old Babylonian Period*', Encyclopedia Britannica Online (22 October 2019), https://www.britannica.com/place/Mesopotamia-historical-region-Asia#ref55481.

El-Kammash, M. M. et al., '*Nile River*', Encyclopedia Britannica Online (9 November 2020), https://www.britannica.com/place/Nile-River.

Emba, E., '*Indonesia's Haze: Should the Victims Pay the Polluters?*', The Diplomat (15 July 2016), https://thediplomat.com/2016/07/indonesias-haze-should-the-victims-pay-the-polluters/.

Encyclopedia Britannica Editors, '*Mount Ararat*', Encyclopedia Britannica Online (23 October 2019), https://www.britannica.com/place/Mount-Ararat.

Epstein, K., '*A Drought Revealed a Palace Thousands of Years Old Submerged in an Iraq Reservoir*', The Washington Post (30 June 2019).

European Court of Human Rights (ECHR), 'An Application Concerning the Potential Impact of Construction of the Ilisu Dam on the Hasankeyf Archaeological Site: Inadmissible', Press Release ECHR 072 (2019) (21 February 2019).

European Parliament, Resolution of 10 February 2010 on Turkey's progress report 2009, P7_TA(2010)0025.

Eyler, B., 'Science Shows Chinese Dams are Devastating the Mekong', *Foreign Policy* (22 April 2020).

FAO, *AQUASTAT Transboundary River Basin Overview—Euphrates-Tigris* (Rome: FAO, 2009).

FAO, *AQUASTAT Transboundary River Basin Overview—Mekong* (Rome: FAO, 2011).

FAO, 'Euphrates-Tigris River Basin', FAO Aquastat (2009), http://www.fao.org/nr/water/aquastat/basins/euphrates-tigris/Euphrates.tigris-CP_eng.pdf.

FAO, 'Euphrates-Tigris: Water Development in the Basin', FAO Aquastat (2016), http://www.fao.org/NR/water/aquastat/countries_regions/profile_segments/euphrates.tigris-IrrDr_eng.stm.

FAO, 'Iraq', FAO Aquastat (2008), http://www.fao.org/nr/water/aquastat/countries_regions/irq/IRQ-CP_eng.pdf.

Fleishman, J., *'Egypt-Ethiopia Water Dispute Escalates After Threatening Remarks'*, The Los Angeles Times (6 June 2013).

Fountain, H., *'Researchers Link Syrian Conflict to a Drought Made Worse by Climate Change'*, The New York Times (2 March 2015).

Frenken, K., *Irrigation Potential in Africa: A Basin Approach* (Rome: Food and Agriculture Organization of the United Nations, 1997).

Gabčíkovo-Nagymaros Project (Hungary/Slovakia), Judgment, ICJ Reports 1997, p. 7.

Gall, C., *'Turkey's President Suffers Stinging Defeat in Istanbul Election Redo'*, The New York Times (23 June 2019).

Gordon, P. E., *Increasing the Share of Renewables in Turkey's Power System: Options for Transmission Expansion and Flexibility* (Istanbul: SHURA Energy Transition Center, 2018).

Greene, B., *'How Did Water Come to Earth?'*, Smithsonian Magazine (May 2013), https://www.smithsonianmag.com/science-nature/how-did-water-come-to-earth-72037248/.

Hadingham, E., *'Where is the Birthplace of Humankind? South Africa and East Africa Both Have Claims'*, National Geographic (11 September 2015), https://www.nationalgeographic.com/news/2015/09/150911-hominin-hominid-berger-homo-naledi-fossils-ancestor-rising-star-human-origins/.

Hammer, J., *'Is a Lack of Water to Blame for the Conflict in Syria?'*, Smithsonian Magazine (June 2013), https://www.smithsonianmag.com/innovation/is-a-lack-of-water-to-blame-for-the-conflict-in-syria-72513729/.

Heidler, J. T., and D. S. Heidler, *'Manifest Destiny'*, Encyclopedia Britannica Online (18 November 2020), https://www.britannica.com/event/Manifest-Destiny.

Hersher, R., *'U.S. Formally Begins to Leave the Paris Climate Agreement'*, National Public Radio (4 November 2019), https://www.npr.org/2019/11/04/773474657/u-s-formally-begins-to-leave-the-paris-climate-agreement.

Hesse, H., *Siddhartha* (New York: New Directions, 1922, 1951).

Hille, K., *'NASA Finds Drought in Eastern Mediterranean Worst of Past 900 Years'*, NASA (1 March 2016), https://www.nasa.gov/feature/goddard/2016/nasa-finds-drought-in-eastern-mediterranean-worst-of-past-900-years.

Hobbs, R. J., *'Intervention Ecology: Applying Ecological Science in the Twenty-first Century'*, 61(6) *BioScience* (2011) 442–450.

Hockenos, P., *'Turkey's Dam Building Spree Continues, at Steep Ecological Cost'*, Yale Environment 360 (3 October 2019), https://e360.yale.edu/features/turkeys-dam-building-spree-continues-at-steep-ecological-cost.

Hubbard, B. G., '*Turkey Launches Offensive against U.S. Backed Syrian Militia*', The New York Times (9 October 2019).

Human Rights Watch, *The Iraqi Government Assault on the Marsh Arabs*, Briefing Paper (January 2003), https://www.hrw.org/legacy/backgrounder/mena/marsharabs1.htm.

Human Rights Watch, '*Turkey/Syria: Weaponizing Water in a Global Pandemic?*' (31 March 2020), https://www.hrw.org/news/2020/03/31/turkey/syria-weaponizing-water-global-pandemic#.

Husain, F. H., 'The Tigris-Euphrates Basin under Early Modern Ottoman Rule, c. 1534–1830' (Ph.D. dissertation, Georgetown University, 2018).

Ilisu Dam Campaign, *Review of EIAR for the Ilisu Dam and HEPP* (2001).

Individuals with Disabilities Education Act, 101st United States Congress (18 June 1990).

International Law Association (ILA), *Report of the Fifty-second Conference, Helsinki* (London: ILA, 1966).

International Rivers, '*Victory: European Governments Backing out of Ilisu Dam Project in Turkey*' (22 June 2009), https://archive.internationalrivers.org/de/node/3535.

Issa, P., '*Rains Like no other: Iraq is Tested in Era of Climate Change*', Associate Press (2 May 2019).

Jacobsen, T., & R. Adams, '*Salt and Silt in Ancient Mesopotamian Agriculture*', 128(3334) Science (21 November 1958) 1251–1257.

Kalpakian, J., *Identity, Conflict and Cooperation in International River Systems* (Routledge, 2017).

Katz, B., '*Turkey is Moving Forward with Plans to Flood a 10,000 Year Old City*', Smithsonian Magazine (12 September 2019), https://www.smithsonianmag.com/smart-news/turkey-moving-forward-its-plans-flood-10000-year-old-city-180973124/.

Kaya, I., '*The Euphrates-Tigris Basin: An Overview and Opportunities for Cooperation under International Law*', Arid Lands Newsletter (Fall/Winter 1998), https://cals.arizona.edu/OALS/ALN/aln44/kaya.html.

Kelley, C. E. et al., 'Climate Change in the Fertile Crescent and Implications of the Recent Syrian Drought', 112(11) *PNAS* (17 March 2015) 3241–3246.

King, L. W. (translator), *The Code of Hammurabi*, The Avalon Project, Yale Law School Lillian Goldman Law Library, https://avalon.law.yale.edu/ancient/hamframe.asp.

Kirschner, A., & K. Tiroch, '*The Waters of the Euphrates and Tigris: An International Law Perspective*', 16 Max Planck Yearbook of United Nations Law (2012) 329–394.

Kornfeld, I., '*Mesopotamia: A History of Water and Law*', in J. Dellapenna & J. Gupta (eds.), *The Evolution of the Law and Politics of Water* (Cham: Springer, 2009), 21–36.

Kubba, S., *The Iraqi Marshlands and the Marsh Arabs* (Trans Pacific Press, 2011).

Kucukgocmen, A., '*Turkey Starts Filling Huge Tigris River Dam, Activists Say*', Reuters (2 August 2019), https://www.reuters.com/article/us-turkey-dam/turkey-starts-filling-huge-tigris-river-dam-activists-say-idUSKCN1US194.

Kucukgocmen, A., '*Turkey to Start Power Generation in Huge Tigris Dam Next Week, Erdogan Says*', Reuters (11 May 2020), https://www.reuters.com/article/us-turkey-dam/turkey-to-start-power-generation-in-huge-tigris-dam-next-week-erdogan-says-idUSKBN22N2L7.

Langcang-Mekong Cooperation China Secretariat, '*A Brief Introduction of Lancang-Mekong Cooperation*' (13 December 2017), http://www.lmcchina.org/eng/gylmhz_1/jj/t1519110.htm.

Letsch, C., '*Turkey's 12,000 Year Old Hasankeyf Settlement Faces Obliteration*', The Guardian (29 August 2017).

Loftas, T., *Dimensions of Need: An Atlas of Food and Agriculture* (Rome: Food and Agriculture Organization of the United Nations, 1995), http://www.fao.org/3/u8480e/U8480E0c.htm#Where%20the%20water%20is.

Magdy, S., '*Egypt, Sudan Suspend Talks with Ethiopia over Disputed Dam*', Associated Press (5 August 2020), https://apnews.com/article/ethiopia-sudan-middle-east-africa-egypt-b8fb2ee6360473cf6c7e28919410ecd6.

Magdy, S., '*Egypt, Ethiopia, Sudan Resume AU-Led Talks over Disputed Dam*', Associated Press (16 August 2020), https://apnews.com/article/addis-ababa-sudan-middle-east-africa-ethiopia-4f09ddb6a500e2617685d78f102a35d0.

Matheson, R., '*Iraq Close to Running Out of Water*', Al Jazeera (18 September 2018).

Mbengue, M. M., '*A Model for African Shared Water Resources: The Senegal River Legal System*', 23(1) Review of European Community & International Environmental Law (2014) 59–66.

McCaffrey, S. C., 'The Law of International Watercourses: Some Recent Developments and Unanswered Questions', 17 *Denver Journal of International Law and Policy* (1989) 505–526.

McCaffrey, S. C., 'The Harmon Doctrine One Hundred Years Later: Buried, Not Praised', 36 *Natural Resources Journal* (1996) 965–1007.

McCaffrey, S. C., 'The Contribution of the UN Convention on the Law of the Non-Navigational Uses of International Watercourses', 1(3–4) *International Journal for Global Environmental Issues* (2001) 250–263.

McCaffrey, S. C., *The Law of International Watercourses* (Oxford: Oxford University Press, 2007).

McCaffrey, S. C., 'The Human Right to Water: A False Promise?', 47 University of the Pacific Law Review (2016) 221–232.

Metropolitan Museum of Art (2000, October). *Heilbrunn Timeline of Art History Mesopotamia 8000–2000 BC*. Retrieved from Metmuseum.org: https://www.metmuseum.org/toah/ht/02/wam.html.

Money, R., '*The Hindiya Barrage, Mesopotamia*', 50(3) The Geographical Journal (1917) 217–222.

Myers, J., '*What is the Anthropocene? And Why Does it Matter?*', World Economic Forum (31 August 2016), https://www.weforum.org/agenda/2016/08/what-is-the-anthropocene-and-why-does-it-matter/.

Naff, T. M., *Water in the Middle East* (Boulder: Westview Press, 1984).

Nahlik, A. M., & M. S. Fennessy, 'Carbon Storage in US Wetlands', 7 *Nature Communications* (2016) article number 13835.

Nam, H., '*Mekong Delta Struggles to Find Freshwater as Drought, Salt Intrusion Continue*', VNExpress International (22 March 2020), https://e.vnexpress.net/news/news/mekong-delta-struggles-to-find-freshwater-as-drought-salt-intrusion-continue-4071219.html.

NASA, 'Drought in Iraq', Visible Earth (1 June 2008), https://visibleearth.nasa.gov/view.php?id=8797.

Nasser, K., '*The Modality of Climate Change in the Middle East, Drought or Drying Up?*', 2(1) *Journal of Interrupted Studies* (2019) 118–140.

Nile Basin Initiative, NBI Overview (1999). Available at, https://nilebasin.org/documents-publications/73-nile-basin-initiative-an-overview/file.

Ohara, N. E., et al., 'Water Balance Study for the Tigris Euphrates River Basin', 16(12) *Journal of Hydrologic Engineering* (2011) 1071–1082.

Osman, T., '*Why Borderlines Drawn with a Ruler in WWI Still Rock the Middle East*', BBC News (14 December 2013), https://www.bbc.com/news/world-middle-east-25299553.

Owen, L. et al., '*Tigris-Euphrates River System*', Encyclopedia Britannica Online (20January2016),https://www.britannica.com/place/Tigris-Euphrates-river-system.

Palmer, M. A., & J. B. Ruhl, '*Aligning Restoration Science and the Law to Sustain Ecological Infrastructure for the Future*', 13(9) Frontiers in Ecology and the Environment (2015) 512–519.

Pamuk, H., '*Turkey Stopped Purchasing Iranian Oil as of May: Turkish Official*', Reuters (22 May 2019), https://www.reuters.com/article/us-turkey-oil-iran-idUSKCN1SS2Z9.

Parker, L., '*3D-Printed Reefs Offer Hope in Coral Bleaching Crisis*', National Geographic (2017).

Parnall, T., & A. E. Utton, '*The Senegal Valley Authority: A Unique Experiment in International River Basin Planning*', 51(2) Indiana Law Journal (1976) 235–256.

Patel, K., '*Slowly Flooding History*', NASA Earth Observatory (2020), https://earthobservatory.nasa.gov/images/146439/slowly-flooding-history.

Popovich, N. et al., '*The Trump Administration is Reversing 100 Environmental Rules. Here's the Full List*', The New York Times (15 July 2020).

Pring, G. R., & B. S. Banaei, 'Tigris and Euphrates Rivers', *Max Planck Encyclopedia of International Law* (2008).

Protocol on matters pertaining to economic cooperation between the Syrian Arab Republic and the Republic of Turkey, signed and in force 17 July 1987, 1724 UNTS 3 (1993).

Pulp Mills on the River Uruguay (Argentina v. Uruguay), Judgment, ICJ Reports 2010, p. 14.

Qureshi, W. A., *'Equitable Apportionment of Shared Transboundary River Waters: A Case Study of Modifications of the Indus Waters Treaty'*, 18 San Diego International Law Journal (2017) 199–240.

Republic of Turkey Ministry of Foreign Affairs. (n.d.). *Turkey's Policy of Water Issues.* Retrieved from Republic of Turkey Ministry of Foreign Affairs: http://www.mfa.gov.tr/turkey_s-policy-on-water-issues.en.mfa.

Richardson, C. H., & N. A. Hussain, 'Restoring the Garden of Eden: An Ecological Assessment of the Marshes of Iraq', 56(6) *BioScience* (2006) 477–489.

Roach, J., *'Amazon Longer than Nile River, Scientists Say'*, National Geographic (2007).

Rocchio, L., *'Turkish Glaciers Shrink by Half'*, NASA Global Climate Change (1 July 2015), https://climate.nasa.gov/news/2304/turkish-glaciers-shrink-by-half/.

Roston, E., & Bloomberg, *'While Most Industries Suffer Due to the Climate Crisis, Hydropower Sees Opportunities'*, Fortune (17 November 2019), https://fortune.com/2019/11/17/climate-change-effects-melting-glaciers-dams-hydropower-freshwater-storage/.

Salman, S. M. A., 'The Helsinki Rules, the UN Watercourses Convention and the Berlin Rules: Perspectives on International Water Law', 23(4) International Journal of Water Resources Development (2007) 625–640.

Salman, S. M. A., *The World Bank Policy for Projects on International Waterways: An Historical and Legal Analysis* (Washington, D.C.: The World Bank, 2009).

Salman, S. M. A., *'How and Why Has the Ethiopian Strategy on Renaissance Dam Succeeded?'*, The Citizen (29 March 2015).

Salman, S. M. A., *'Notification Concerning Planned Measures on Shared Watercourses,'* 4(2) Brill Research Perspectives in International Water Law (2020).

Sand, P. H., *'Mesopotamia 2550 B.C.: The Earliest Boundary Water Treaty'*, 5(4) Global Journal of Archaeology and Anthropology (2018).

Sasipornkarn, E., *'A Dam-building Race Threatens the Mekong'*, Deutsche Welle (16 August 2019), https://www.dw.com/en/about-dw/profile/s-30688.

Sattar, O., *'Iraq Fears Bevy of Levees Will Mean Parched Years Ahead'*, *AL-Monitor* (5 April 2019).

Save the Tigris and Iraqi Marshes Campaign, *'Ilisu Dam and Legal Considerations in Iraq'*, Policy paper presented to the Iraqi government (22 March 2014), https://www.iraqicivilsociety.org//wp-content/uploads/2014/04/ILISU-DAM-AND-LEGAL-CONSIDERATIONS-IN-IRAQ-Eng.pdf.

Segreti, G., *'Pope Francis Calls for Dialogue between Egypt, Ethiopia and Sudan over Nile Dam'*, Reuters (15 August 2020), https://www.reuters.com/article/us-ethiopia-dam-pope-idUSKCN25B0KJ.

Sevinclidir, P., *'Hasankeyf: Ancient Town in Turkey Faces Dam Flood'*, BBC News Online (2 February 2016), https://www.bbc.com/news/world-middle-east-35471815.

Snyder, J., '*The Broken Bargain: How Nationalism Came Back*', Foreign Affairs (March/April 2019).

Statute of the River Uruguay, adopted 26 February 1975, in force 18 September 1976, 1295 UNTS 331.

Tadesee, A. G., '*Ethiopia Showcases First Locally-Assembled Electric Car*', Andalou Agency (27 July 2020), https://www.aa.com.tr/en/africa/ethiopia-showcases-first-locally-assembled-electric-car/1924109.

Tanner, J. F., *The Internally Displaced People of Iraq* (The Brookings Institution, 2002).

Taylor, A., '*Artificial Reefs around the World*', The Atlantic (2011).

Tekuya, M. E., '*The Egyptian Hydro Hegemony in the Nile Basin: The Quest for Changing the Status Quo*', 26(1) Journal of Water Law (2018) 10–20.

The Indus Waters Treaty 1960 between the Government of India, the Government of Pakistan and the International Bank for Reconstruction and Development, adopted 19 September 1960, in force 12 January 1961, 419 UNTS 125.

The New York Times, '"Attorney General Judson Harmon" reproduced from The Cincinnati Commercial Gazette (11 June 1895)', https://www.nytimes.com/1895/06/11/archives/attorney-general-judson-harmon.html.

The World Bank, 'The World Bank in China', https://www.worldbank.org/en/country/china/overview.

Treaty of Friendship and Neighbourly Relations between Iraq and Turkey, signed 29 March 1946, 37 UNTS 226.

Treaty of Lausanne, The Convention Respecting the Regime of the Straits and Instruments Signed at Lausanne, signed 24 July 1923.

Treaty on the Delimitation of the Frontiers between Ethiopia and Sudan, adopted 15 May 1902, Addis Ababa, Ethiopia.

Turkish Ministry of Foreign Affairs, *Water: A Source of Conflict or Cooperation in the Middle East?*, http://www.mfa.gov.tr/data/DISPOLITIKA/WaterASourceofConflictofCoopintheMiddleEast.pdf.

United Nations Conference on the Environment and Development, *Rio Declaration on Environment and Development*, UN Doc A/CONF.151/26/Rev.1 (Vol. I) (12 August 1992), Annex I.

United Nations Economic and Social Commission for Western Asia (UN-ESCWA) & Bundesanstalt für Geowissenschaften und Rohstoffe (BGR), *Inventory of Shared Water Resources in Western Asia* (Beirut: UN-ESCWA and BGR, 2013).

United Nations Economic and Social Council, General Comment No. 15 (2002): The right to water (arts 11 and 12 of the International Covenant on Economic, Social and Cultural Rights), UN Doc. E/C.12/2002/11 (20 January 2003).

United Nations Educational, Scientific and Cultural Organization, *Integrated Drought Risk Management—National Framework for Iraq* (Baghdad: UNESCO, 2014).

United Nations Educational, Scientific and Cultural Organization, *Report of the Decisions adopted during the 40th session of the World Heritage Committee (Istanbul/ UNESCO, 2016*), Doc. WHC/16/40.COM/19 (15 November 2016), Decision: 40 COM 8B.16, at 201–205.

United Nations Environment Programme, '*Ethiopia Plants over 350 Million Trees in a Day, Setting New World Record*' (2 August 2019), https://www.unenvironment.org/news-and-stories/story/ethiopia-plants-over-350-million-trees-day-setting-new-world-record.

United Nations General Assembly, Press Release GA/9248, 99th Meeting (AM) 21 May 1997, https://www.internationalwaterlaw.org/documents/intldocs/convention_press.html.

United Nations General Assembly, Resolution 64/292 The human right to water, adopted 28 July 2010, UN Doc. A/RES/64/292 (3 August 2010).

United Nations High Commissioner for Refugees (UNHCR), *Evaluation of UNHCR's Emergency Response to the Influx of Syrian Refugees into Turkey January 2014–June 2015* (Geneva: UN High Commissioner for Refugees, 2015).

United Nations, International Covenant on Economic, Social and Cultural Rights, adopted 16 December 1966, in force 3 January 1976, 993 UNTS 3.

United Nations Security Council, Resolution 687 adopted 3 April 1991, UN Doc. S/RES/687 (1991) (8 April 1991).

United Nations Security Council, Note by the President of the Security Council, UN Doc. S/23500 (31 January 1992).

United Nations Watercourses Convention, 'User's Guide Factsheet Series Number 10: Theories of Resource Allocation', https://www.unwatercoursesconvention.org/documents/UNWC-Fact-Sheet-10-Theories-of-Resource-Allocation.pdf.

United States Department of State, Office of the Historian, 'Papers Relating to the Foreign Relations of the United States, 1894, With the Annual Message of the President, Transmitted to Congress, December 3, 1894', https://history.state.gov/historical documents/frus1894/d386.

United States Institute of Peace, '*The Marsh Arabs of Iraq: Hussein's Lesser Known Victims*', Press Release (November 25 2002), https://www.usip.org/press/2002/11/marsh-arabs-iraq-husseins-lesser-known-victims.

University of Alberta, '*Reimbursing Ranchers for Livestock Killed by Predators Supports Conservation Efforts: Compensation Program Offsets Costs of Preserving Wildlife Habitat on Private Land*', Science Daily (17 January 2018), https://www.sciencedaily.com/releases/2018/01/180117152459.htm.

Ünver, O., & A. Kibaroglu, '*An Institutional Framework for Facilitating Cooperation in the Euphrates-Tigris River Basin*', 5(2) International Negotiations (2000) 311–330.

von Hein, M., '*Weaponizing Water in Northern Syria?*', Deutsche Welle (25 March 2020), https://p.dw.com/p/3a2QU.

Walsh, D., '*As Egypt's Population Hits 100 Million, Celebration is Muted*', The New York Times (11 February 2020).

Walsh, D., '*As Seasonal Rains Fall, Dispute Over Nile Dam Rushes Toward a Reckoning*', The New York Times (18 July 2020).

Walsh, D., & S. Sengupta, '*For Thousands of Years, Egypt Controlled the Nile. A New Dam Threatens That*', The New York Times (9 February 2020).

Walton, B., '*New Bank Loans Revive Controversial Ilisu Dam Project in Turkey*', Circle of Blue, (13 January 2010), https://www.circleofblue.org/2010/world/new-bank-loans-revive-controversial-ilisu-dam-project-in-turkey/.

Wilks, A. (2019, October 7). History Threatened as Turkey Prepares to Flood Ancient City. *Aljazzera*.

Wolf, A., *Middle East Water Conflicts and Directions for Conflict Resolution* (Washington, D.C.: International Food Policy Research Center, 1 Protocol on matters pertaining to economic cooperation between the Syrian Arab Republic and the Republic of Turkey, signed and in force 17 July 1987, 1724 UNTS 3 (1993)996).

Wu, S., '*The Trouble with the Lancang Mekong Cooperation Forum*', The Diplomat (19 December 2018), https://thediplomat.com/2018/12/the-trouble-with-the-lancang-mekong-cooperation-forum/.

Youness, M. A., '*How Climate Change Contributed to the Conflicts in the Middle East and North Africa*', World Bank Arab Voices blog (10 December 2015), https://blogs.worldbank.org/arabvoices/climate-change-conflict-mena.

Zeitoun, M., & J. Warner, '*Hydro-Hegemony—A Framework for Analysis of Trans-Boundary Water Conflicts*', 8 *Water Policy* (2006) 435–460.

www.ingramcontent.com/pod-product-compliance
Lightning Source LLC
Chambersburg PA
CBHW031330230926
51848CB00001B/174